SOS Help For Parents:
A Practical Guide For Handling Common Everyday Behavior Problems

THIRD EDITION

www.sosprograms.com

Also in Spanish!

**See DVD/Video clips in English & Spanish at
www.sosprograms.com**

The DVD/Video SOS Help For Parents

A DVD/Video-Discussion Parent Education
& Counseling Program (English & Spanish)

For parenting workshops, staff development,
in-service training, churches,
classroom use, and counseling.
See pages 205 – 208 and 247 – 249

*"The multi-media approach [of SOS Help For Parents
Program] makes the information accessible to
parents and children at all levels of adjustment
and functioning,"*
  – Journal Of Marital And Family Therapy

SOS – A Practical
Multicultural Parenting Program

*"I utilized your book with excellent results with
children and their parents when I was in
Connecticut. Currently I am in Istanbul, Turkey
and have found your book quite helpful with
Turkish parents as well."*
  – Yanki Yazgan, MD, Child Psychiatry, Marmara,
University, Istanbul, Turkey

Read SOS Help For Parents!

Manage your children before they manage you!

SOS Help For Parents can help you to:

- **Improve your parenting skills**
- **Improve your self-confidence**
- **Improve your child's emotional adjustment**
- **Improve your relationship with your child**
- **Reduce stress in your life**

READ WHAT OTHERS ARE SAYING ABOUT SOS!

- *"SOS is an extremely comprehensive book. . . an excellent book. We highly recommend it."*
  – Journal of Clinical Child Psychology

- *"Lynn Clark drew on his 20 years of working with parents and children when he wrote SOS Help For Parents."*
  – USA Today

- *"SOS turned our family around... I really regained my self-confidence as a parent."*
  – Mother of two, Riverview, Michigan

- *"It's a wonderful book...easy to read, simple, and based on sound research."*
  – Emel Summer, MD, Director of Child Psychiatry,
    DePaul Health Center, St. Louis, Missouri

- *"...a superb book for parents (and for professionals)."*
  – Dr. David DeLawyer, Psychologist - Tacoma, Washington

- *"SOS... cannot help but make a parent's life easier and more enjoyable. I endorse it with enthusiasm!"*
  – A. J. Moser, Director - Center For Human Potential

- *"...easy to read and its content is excellent."*
  – Contemporary Psychology Journal

by Lynn Clark, Ph.D.

SOS Behavior Management & Parenting Programs

SOS Help For Parents: A Practical Guide For Handling Common Everyday Behavior Problems.

English edition	SOS Programs & Parents Press
Spanish edition	SOS Programs & Parents Press
Korean edition	Kyoyuk-Kwahak-Sa, Ltd.
Chinese edition	Beijing Normal University Press
Chinese edition	Taiwan, Psychological Co., Ltd.
Turkish edition	Evrim Yaymevi ve Tic.Ltd. Co.
Hungarian edition	Budapest, Pedagogia Szervezet
Icelandic edition	University of Iceland
Arabic edition	Yousef Abuhmaiden, Alkerak, Jordan
Japanese edition	Tokyo Tosho
Portuguese edition	Editora Cognitiva
Dutch Edition	Bohn Stafleu van Loghum
Estonian edition	Ersen Ou Eram Books

> Free Video Clips & Resources
> **www.sosprograms.com**

DVD Video SOS Help For Parents education program

English edition	SOS Programs & Parents Press
Spanish edition	SOS Programs & Parents Press
Hungarian edition	Budapest, Pedagogia Szervezet
Icelandic edition	University of Iceland

How To Use Time-Out Effectively audio CD program

> *SOS Help For Emotions* is a self-help book, not a parenting book.

SOS Help For Emotions: Managing Anxiety, Anger, And Depression. Second Edition

English edition	SOS Programs & Parents Press
Spanish edition	SOS Programs & Parents Press
Turkish edition	Evrim Yaymevi ve Tic.Ltd. Co.
Korean edition	Kyoyuk-Kwahak-Sa, Ltd.
Chinese edition	Beijing Normal University Press
Japanese edition	Tokyo Tosho

English SOS

SOS Help For Parents
13 International
Editions
and Languages

Portuguese, Dutch (The Netherlands), and Estonian are additional editions.

Spanish SOS

Turkish SOS

Japanese SOS

Chinese SOS
Beijing Normal Univ

Korean SOS

Chinese SOS
Taiwan

Hungarian SOS

Arabic SOS

Icelandic SOS

Read

SOS Help For Emotions:
Managing Anxiety, Anger
And Depression

> **Manage your emotions
> before
> they manage you!**

SOS Help For Emotions can help you to:
- Know your emotions
- Manage your emotions
- Manage your relationships
- Attain greater contentment
- Achieve your personal goals
- Enhance your emotional intelligence

SOS Help For Parents:
A Practical Guide For Handling Common Everyday Behavior Problems

THIRD EDITION

Lynn Clark, Ph.D.

SOS Programs & Parents Press
PO Box 2180
Bowling Green, KY. 42102-2180 U.S.A.
www.sosprograms.com

SOS Help For Parents:
A Practical Guide For Handling Common Everyday Behavior Problems

THIRD EDITION

Copyright © 2005 by Lynn Clark
With 2010 Revisions

Publisher's Cataloging-In-Publication Data

Clark, Lynn, date.
   SOS help for parents : a practical guide for handling common everyday behavior problems / [by Lynn Clark ; illustrations by John Robb].— 3rd ed.

   p. : ill. ; cm.
   Includes bibliographical references and index.
   ISBN-10: 0-935111-21-2   ISBN-13: 978-0-935111-21-7

1. Discipline of children. 2. Child rearing. 3. Timeout method. I. Robb, John. II. Title. III. Title: Help for parents

HQ770.4 .C52 2005
649/.64   2005908084

Printed in the United States of America

Published by: SOS Programs & Parents Press
               Post Office Box 2180
               Bowling Green, KY 42102-2180 USA
               Tele: 270-842-4571   Toll free: 1-800-576-1582
               Fax: 270-796-9194
               website www.sosprograms.com

15 14 13 12 11 10 9 8 7 6 5 4 3

DEDICATION

To children and those who rear them

Publisher's Note

WARNING

This book is designed to provide information in regard to the subject matter covered. It is sold with the understanding that the publisher and author are not engaged in rendering psychological, medical, or other professional services.

Rearing children is sometimes very difficult. If expert assistance is needed, seek the services of a competent professional. Chapter 22 describes how to obtain professional help.

Counselors often ask parents to read SOS in conjunction with parent education and parent counseling.

ACKNOWLEDGMENTS — First Edition

I am especially indebted to Gerald Patterson, Rex Forehand, and their colleagues for much of this book's research and clinical foundations. Donald Baer introduced me to behavioral child management research when I was a graduate student at The University of Kansas. B. F. Skinner, for more than a half-century, has contributed fundamental research on human behavior and also kindly gave his permission to use the cartoon illustration in Chapter 22.

Gerald Patterson at the Oregon Social Learning Center and Mark Roberts at Idaho State University reviewed the manuscript. Their comments and recommendations improved the usefulness of SOS.

Carole Clark critiqued each of the many manuscript drafts and contributed true examples of problem behaviors and parent-child interactions. Mary Ann Kearny and Virginia Lezhnev made suggestions regarding writing style and provided encouragement.

Individuals at Western Kentucky University who contributed to SOS include Patrice Nolan, Lois Layne, Clinton Layne, Harry Robe, William Pfohl, Elsie Dotson, Ned Kearny, Fred Stickle, Livingston Alexander, Carl Martray, Delbert Hayden, and James Warwick. Many graduate and undergraduate students also contributed useful comments regarding the manuscript.

John Robb contributed expert illustrations.

Copyreading was done by Beverly Cravens. Janet Allen helped type the manuscript revisions. Bettye Neblett offered valuable suggestions regarding SOS and provided swift, expert typing.

ACKNOWLEDGMENTS — Second Edition

My two sons were children when I wrote the first edition of *SOS Help For Parents*, and they are now adults. Revising SOS has been a family project in many ways.

Eric critiqued most of the revised chapters and made many valuable comments. Todd retyped the first edition of SOS into a professional word processing program so that I could more easily prepare the second edition. Carole Clark critiqued each of the revised chapters so that the ideas would be clearer.

SOS readers, including parents, teachers, and mental health professionals, have offered many reactions regarding the first edition and contributed ideas for the second edition. SOS and I are indebted to all these individuals.

ACKNOWLEDGMENTS — Third Edition

I appreciate the useful and positive feedback that I have received from the many parents, educators, mental health professionals, graduate students, and physicians over the years. SOS is now available in eight languages and additional translations are in progress. Over 10,000 copies of *The Video SOS Help For Parents* educational program have been used by mental health professionals and educators around the world to educate and counsel parents.

The SOS Help For Parents program continues to evolve and develop new training components, all with the ultimate objective of helping parents and children. I make additional improvements and updates to SOS each time that it is printed.

I particularly appreciate the continuing support that Carole, Eric, and Todd have given in further developing SOS.

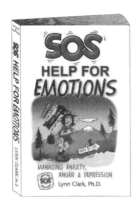

SOS Help For Emotions:
Managing Anxiety, Anger, & Depression!

READ WHAT OTHERS ARE SAYING:

"Beautifully captures the spirit of Rational Emotive Behavior Therapy in concise, evocative, and humorous language. A gem of an introduction to REBT."
> – Albert Ellis, Ph.D., President of Albert Ellis Institute and author of *A Guide to Rational Living.*

"SOS is a beautiful work! The use of cartoons, figures, and illustrations is quite engaging."
> – Donald Beal, Ph.D., Associate Professor of Psychology, Eastern Kentucky University.

"It's spectacular! SOS is the best self-help book on Rational Emotive Behavior Therapy that I have seen."
> – Raymond DiGiuseppe, Ph.D., Past President, Association for Behavioral and Cognitive Therapies (ABCT).

Manage Your Emotions, Relationships, and Life!

SOS Help For Emotions is a self-help book, not a parenting book.

CONTENTS

Section Four
MORE RESOURCES FOR HELPING YOUR CHILD

"Happy together!"

SOS Help For Parents:
A Practical Guide For Handling Common Everyday Behavior Problems

THIRD EDITION

www.sosprograms.com

SOS Help For Emotions:
Managing Anxiety, Anger, And Depression

Self-Help and Cognitive Behavior Therapy for ages 14 to 90

International Editions
and Languages

English SOS

Spanish SOS

Turkish SOS

Chinese SOS

Korean SOS

Japanese SOS

Read sample chapters at www.sosprograms.com

INTRODUCTION

JESSICA

"I always win!"

Six-year-old Jessica was out of control. When angry, she bit her wrist till it bled, screamed and swore, hit her mother or attacked a wall or door in a fit of rage! Jessica *always* insisted on having her own way. Once at a shopping center, she refused to accompany her parents back to their car. Instead, she forced them to chase her through parked cars and traffic. Severe scoldings and spankings were ineffective in stopping her from behaving like a brat. Jessica was in charge.

Early in my experience as a psychologist, I worked with Jessica and Mrs. Stiles, her mother. Mrs. Stiles agreed to try counseling although she was pessimistic about changing her daughter. I didn't work directly with Jessica. Instead, I taught Mrs. Stiles effective methods of discipline and child management. She correctly applied these methods, and after a stormy eight weeks, Jessica's behavior changed dramatically. She didn't become an angel, but she became manageable.

During our counseling sessions, Mrs. Stiles was always a little upset with me. She was annoyed that I gave professional advice in managing Jessica when I had no children of my own. Also, she felt that I hadn't fully appreciated how difficult it was being Jessica's mother.

Several months after we concluded parent counseling, Mrs. Stiles learned that my wife was expecting our first child.

What was Mrs. Stiles' reaction upon hearing the good news? She exclaimed, *"I hope that Dr. Clark's kid is as mean as a snake! Then he'll know what I had to put up with!"*

Although you may not have a "Jessica," chances are that you do have a child who isn't always an angel. *SOS Help For Parents* can help you to become a more self-confident and effective parent. You'll learn many new methods for improving your child's behavior. As a result, your child will be better behaved and happier. You life will be simpler and more pleasant.

This book is your guide for handling a variety of common behavior problems. We'll look at specific solutions to problems such as the following:

Problems Parents Face

• Your three-year-old hits you when he doesn't get his way. You have tried scolding and spanking but his behavior is getting worse.

• It embarrasses and angers you when your ten-year-old daughter talks back to you whenever you ask her to do a simple chore. When you explain to her how impolite her "back-talk" is, she mocks you.

• You dread Saturday mornings. Your twelve-year-old and eight-year-old regularly engage in Saturday morning arguing and fighting while watching television. You repeatedly warn them to stop arguing and fighting. But really you have nothing effective to back up your warnings.

• Your five-year-old daughter has started having tantrums. She is even having tantrums in the homes of your friends. You are tired of her behavior and tired of making excuses for her. You feel helpless to change her.

The behavioral approach to child rearing and discipline is very useful in understanding children and helping them to change. What is the behavioral approach? What is behavioral discipline? *The behavioral approach states that good and bad behavior are both learned.* It also maintains that behavior can be "unlearned" or changed. *Behavioral discipline* offers tested methods, skills, procedures, and strategies for you to use in getting improved behavior from your child.

You can be optimistic about helping your child to change. Behavioral methods are extremely effective in changing all kinds of problem behavior. Child research studies conducted in the United States and other countries show a 50 to 90 percent reduction in a wide variety of problem behaviors with the use of behavioral methods. As a parent and psychologist, I have considerable confidence in these methods. In fact, I have used nearly all the behavioral methods described in this book with my own children. These skills are easy to learn, and they work.

"No one told us that it would be like this!"

How To Use This Book

Read chapters 1 through 12 before you actually begin using these new strategies with your child. Understanding the methods, step-by-step instructions, and examples in these chapters will enable you to be successful in guiding your child to improved behavior. Also, you will learn to avoid common pitfalls and mistakes when managing your child.

At the end of each chapter is a section called "Main Points To Remember." These are the most important ideas and instructions contained in each chapter.

SOS Help for Parents is based on my professional practice as a psychologist, my personal experience as a parent, and the conclusions of numerous parent-child research studies.

Managing one's children is a challenging and sometimes humbling task, even for psychologists and family counselors. My wife (an elementary teacher) and I began to use the methods of discipline and child management described in this book with our two sons when they were toddlers.

Many years after working with Mrs. Stiles and Jessica, I still think about Mrs. Stiles and her "good wishes" for my firstborn! I have continued to study child management, not only to help parents, but because I certainly didn't want to be cursed with *"a kid as mean as a snake!"*

My purposes in writing SOS are to help parents to be better parents and to help children to be more competent and better adjusted. As a clinical psychologist, I am aware of tested methods for helping parents and children, and I want to make these methods and skills known to many parents.

Tested methods for helping children are based on research studies conducted throughout the world. SOS methods are multicultural; these methods for helping children can be applied by parents from various cultural backgrounds. SOS is published in eight languages.

SOS Help For Parents has enjoyed enormous success and positive feedback from thousands of parents and professionals. Parents from diverse backgrounds in the United States and in many foreign countries are now using the SOS Parenting Program.

Chapter 1

Why Kids Behave And Misbehave

UNCOOPERATIVE BEHAVIOR

COOPERATIVE BEHAVIOR

"No! . . . I won't do it!"

"Whew! . . . This is hard work."

Why do some children sail through childhood with few noticeable behavior problems, while others are a constant problem to their parents? Children, as well as adults, find these "problem kids" obnoxious and either complain about them or avoid them. It's as though some problem kids lie awake at night plotting their next day's misbehavior.

As a psychologist, I've had a firsthand look at the feelings of frustration and failure which many parents experience. Frustrated parents also lie awake at night, desperate for solutions.

Solutions do exist! With increased knowledge of the rules and methods for improving behavior, you can help your child be a better behaved and more agreeable family member.

Good and bad behavior are both shaped by the rewards your child receives. Sometimes parents "accidentally" reward and strengthen their child's bad behavior. Three-year-old Patrick may get to stay up well past his bedtime (a reward) if he "wears his parents down" with relentless complaining and crying. Your child's bad behavior will grow stronger if you or other people reward it. Behavior that is not rewarded or is corrected, will grow weaker and be less likely to occur in the future.

Follow three basic child rearing rules. The rules *look* simple! You can easily see what your friends are doing wrong with *their* children. However, when you try to use these rules with *your* child, you can appreciate how difficult it is to be consistent and effective. Remember these rules!

Three Child Rearing Rules —

Parents' Check List

Rule #1. Reward good behavior (and do it quickly and often).*

Rule #2. Don't "accidentally" reward bad behavior.**

Rule #3. Correct some bad behavior (but use *mild* correction only).

Rule #1 Reward Good Behavior
(And Do it Quickly And Often)

Children learn to talk, dress themselves, share toys, and do chores because they receive attention and other types of rewards from their parents and other people for doing so. As parents, we should frequently and abundantly reward the good behavior of our children.

An adult holds a job and in return receives a paycheck and recognition from others. A paycheck and recognition are powerful rewards for working. Most of us would stop working if we weren't rewarded for our effort. Rewards shape and determine our behavior and the behavior of our children. Rewards are also called reinforcers because they reinforce behavior.

When your child gets a reward for engaging in a particular

---

*When behavior is rewarded, that behavior receives "positive reinforcement" or simply "reinforcement."

* *When behavior which once was rewarded is no longer rewarded, the term "extinction" is used. Extinction is also called nonreinforcement of behavior.

behavior, that behavior is strengthened or reinforced. This means that the behavior is more likely to occur in the future. People repeat behavior for which they are rewarded. We continue going to work because we get paid. If your child behaves in a way that pleases you, be sure to strengthen that behavior by frequently rewarding it. What type of rewards should you use? Read on!

Social rewards are very effective in strengthening the desirable behavior of both children and adults. Social rewards include smiles, hugs, pats, kisses, words of praise, eye contact, and attention. A hug or a kind word is easy to give. That's good because our children need lots of social rewards to strengthen their appropriate behavior.

Hugs are powerful *social rewards* for children
— and for parents as well.

Some parents are stingy with their praise and attention. They may say that they are too busy or that their child ought to demonstrate good behavior without being rewarded for it. Parents who are stingy with smiles, hugs, and words of praise don't realize the powerful effect of frequently rewarding their child's desirable behavior. If four-year-old Emily straightens her room or helps you with the chores, you need to tell her that you appreciate it. If you don't, she will be less likely to help with chores in the future.

Praise is more effective in strengthening your child's desirable behavior if you praise the specific behavior rather than your child. Descriptive praise is praising the behavior and not the child. After your daughter cleans and straightens her room, use descriptive praise and say, *"Your room looks great and you did such a good job cleaning it!"* That statement of descriptive praise is more effective than saying, *"You are a good girl."* Develop the habit of praising the specific behavior or actions that you want strengthened.

Rewards Children Like

Social Rewards	Activity Rewards Including Privileges	Material Rewards
Smiles	Play cards with mother	Item at grocery
Hugs	Go to park	Ball
Pats	Look at book with father	Money
Attention	Help bake cookies	Book
Touching	Watch a late TV movie	Jump rope
Clap hands	Have a friend over	Balloons
Winks	Play ball with father	Yo-yo
Praise	Play a game together	Flashlight
"Good job"	Go out for pizza together	Special dessert
"Well done"	Play at playground	CD

Besides *social rewards*, you can also give *material rewards* and *activity rewards* such as a special dessert, a small toy, nickels and dimes, a trip to the Dairy Queen, or helping a parent bake a cake. For most children, however, social rewards are much more powerful than material rewards. In addition, social rewards are more convenient for you to use. Remember, you are the main source of rewards for your child.

To be effective, rewards must *immediately* follow the child's desirable behavior. If your daughter takes out the trash (even if that is her regular chore), you should thank her immediately after the task is done — not an hour or so later. All of us like to receive rewards for good behavior as immediately as possible. Children often ask to receive material rewards *before rather than after* they do a chore or engage in a desirable behavior. If you sometimes use material rewards, be sure you give them only *after* the desirable behavior occurs. When you give a material reward or activity reward to your child, also give a social reward.

Rule #2 Don't "Accidentally" Reward Bad Behavior

"ACCIDENTALLY" REWARDING BAD BEHAVIOR

"But, I don't want to go to bed!" I'm not tired . . . ."

"Calm down! You can stay up another 30 minutes. I can't stand to hear you cry and carry on . . . ."

When you accidentally reward your child's misbehavior, that misbehavior is strengthened and is more likely to occur again in the future. Often, busy or preoccupied parents unintentionally reward their child for engaging in undesirable or inappropriate behavior. *When parents reward bad behavior, they are causing future problems for themselves as well as for their children.* This is probably one of the most common child rearing mistakes which parents make.

Teaching Nathan To Whine

When five-year-old Nathan wants his mother's attention, especially when she is busy, he begins to whine. Mother finds his whining so unbearable that she stops whatever she is doing, scolds him for whining, and then asks what is troubling him. Nathan has learned that when he *really* wants his mother's attention, he first must whine and accept a mild scolding. Then he gets his mother's attention — a powerful reward for five-year-old Nathan. Mother has taught Nathan to whine.

Also, *children teach parents to behave in certain ways.* Nathan has taught his mother to give him attention when he whines. When she gives him attention, he rewards her by stopping his whining. *Children and parents "teach" each other both appropriate and inappropriate behaviors.*

Your child may have learned that he can delay going to bed at night by complaining, crying, and becoming emotionally upset when you say it's bedtime. After his complaining and crying have become intolerable, have you ever given in and let him stay up longer? If you have given in, you have unintentionally rewarded him for crying and becoming emotionally upset. Complaining, crying, and getting upset are more likely to occur in the future. These behaviors are learned and reinforced just as appropriate and desirable behaviors are learned and reinforced. Don't reward bad behavior or behavior which you don't want.

The strong-willed child is another example of how parents and others can accidentally reward bad behavior and cause that behavior to become a severe problem. Watching a child cry and have a temper tantrum is distressing and emotionally upsetting. To stop her persistent crying and tantrums, parents and other people eventually give in to her demands. Thus, the strong-willed child learns to force others to give in to her demands by causing them emotional pain and discomfort.*

---

*Children with ADHD (Attention-Deficit/Hyperactivity Disorder), Conduct Disorder, or Oppositional Defiant Disorder usually are particularly strong-willed.

A strong-willed child may achieve considerable power and control over her parents and others. To get her way, she may engage in endless pestering and complaining, yelling and crying, or physical attacks on parents, siblings, and peers. Only when others give her what she wants will she stop causing them stress and emotional pain. With boundless energy and endurance, she forces her parents and others to reward her bad behavior. However, you can help the strong-willed child by using the SOS child management skills outlined in this book.

THE STRONG-WILLED CHILD

"I'm ready to eat NOW!"

The strong-willed child can become skillful and powerful in controlling her parents, siblings, and peers. She uses "control-by-pain."

RULE #3 Correct Some Bad Behavior
(But Use *Mild* Correction Only)

You sometimes need to use *mild* correction to decrease or eliminate some unacceptable or dangerous behavior.

You dislike correcting your child. You would prefer to reward good behavior. However, correctly using *mild* correction is often essential in helping your child. You'll learn about the use of *mild* correction such as scolding, natural consequences, logical consequences, time-out, and behavior penalty. However, don't use *severe* correction, such as grim threats, sarcasm, or hard spankings. This often complicates behavior problems.

Christy Loses Her Tricycle

Mother saw four-year-old Christy ride her new tricycle into the street. That was against the rule and the rule already had been explained to Christy.

Immediately, Mother walked out to the street, removed Christy from her tricycle, and harshly scolded her. Mother also said, "*Christy, for riding in the street — you can't ride your tricycle for a week.*" The tricycle was put away. It was seven days before Christy could play with it again.

Four Child Rearing Errors To Avoid

Do follow the basic child rearing rules discussed previously. Also, avoid making the following four child rearing errors. These parenting errors can contribute to behavior problems or emotional problems in children. Parents as well as children are imperfect, but do the best job of parenting you can!

Examples Of Child Rearing *Errors*

Error #1
Parents Fail To Reward Good Behavior

Example — Brian, a fourth grader, walks up to his father carrying his report card. Father, in his easy chair, is busy reading the newspaper. Father fails to reward his son for getting good grades in school.

Brian: *"I made pretty good grades this term. Would you like to see my report card, Dad?"*

Father: *"Yes, but let me finish reading the paper first . . . Would you go and ask Mother if she paid the bills today?"*

"Accidentally" Causing Behavior Problems — Four Child Rearing *Errors To Avoid*

Error #1. Parents fail to reward good behavior.

Error #2. Parents "accidentally" correct good behavior.

Error #3. Parents "accidentally" reward bad behavior.

Error #4. Parents fail to correct bad behavior (when *mild* correction is indicated).

Error #2
Parents "Accidentally" Correct Good Behavior

Example — Eight-year-old Sarah wants to surprise Mother by washing the lunch dishes. Mother unintentionally corrects her.

Sarah: *"I washed the dishes, Mother. Are you glad?"*

Mother: *"It's about time you did something to help around here. Now, what about the pans on the stove? Did you forget about them? . . ."*

Error #3
Parents "Accidentally" Reward Bad Behavior

Example — Six-year-old Pam and her parents are camping and have just arrived back at camp with groceries for lunch. Mother is hot, tired, and hungry.

Pam: *"I want to go swimming before lunch."*

Mother: *"First we eat lunch and have a nap, then you can go swimming."*

Pam: *"I'll cry if I can't go swimming!"*

Mother *"Oh Pam, anything but that! Go ahead and swim first."*

Error #4
Parents Fail To Correct Bad Behavior
(When *Mild* Correction Is Indicated)

> Example — Mother and Father are sitting in the family room. Both observe eleven-year-old Mark impulsively hit his younger brother on the ear. Neither parent scolds Mark or uses any other form of mild correction for his aggressive behavior.

> Mother: *"I wish you would handle your son."*

> Father: *"Boys will be boys!"*

Physical Problems May Contribute To Behavior Problems

Being hungry or overly tired can temporarily lower your child's capacity for self-control and intensify his bad behavior. Certain medical conditions can also increase the likelihood of behavior problems. If you suspect that your child has a medical condition, take him to your family physician or pediatrician for a checkup.

Even though a chronic physical condition may contribute to your child's bad behavior, keep working on improving that behavior. All the rules and methods discussed in this book are entirely suitable for helping children with handicaps or other physical problems. Succeeding chapters will show you *when and how* to use effective methods for helping your child to improve his behavior.

Main Points To Remember:

- Both good and bad behavior are strengthened when rewarded.

- Reward your child's good behavior quickly and often.

- Avoid rewarding your child's bad behavior.

- Use *mild* correction to decrease or eliminate some behaviors.

The Video SOS Help For Parents, available for parent educators and counselors, teaches the **Three Child Rearing Rules** and the **Four Child Rearing Errors To Avoid**, among other parenting skills. View free video clips at www.sosprograms.com

Chapter 2

Clear Communication Promotes Effective Parenting

PROBLEMS FAMILIES FACE — *POOR COMMUNICATION*

JOHN
ROBB

Mother and father must maintain clear communication between themselves and agree on goals.

Parents must agree about which behaviors are desirable and undesirable for their child. Otherwise, their son or daughter may become confused about what is expected of them and behave badly as a result.

Clear and frequent communication between you and your spouse promotes effective parenting. Likewise, clear communication between you and your child is also essential for helping to improve his behavior. Good communication requires a lot of talking and listening by all family members. Your child needs clear communication, discipline, and love from you.

Parents Must Agree On Goals

You and your spouse must determine which of your child's behaviors are good or desirable and which are bad or undesirable. Your basic values determine the goals and standards of behavior you set for your child. Reward and strengthen your child's good behavior and eliminate or weaken her unacceptable behavior by failing to reward it.

PARENTS SOLVING PROBLEMS

Clear communication between mother and father is important.

Both Rewarding *And* Correcting David's Baby Talk

When four-year-old David wanted something or just wanted attention, he often used "baby talk." If he was thirsty, he would point to the kitchen faucet and say, "wa-wa". David's mother thought his baby talk was cute and often rewarded it (getting him a drink of water when he said, "wa-wa"). David's father thought his baby talk was obnoxious, scolded him for it, and called him a "sissy."

David was being rewarded *and* corrected for using baby talk. As the days passed, David became more and more emotional, cried easily, and began avoiding his father.

Rewarding and correcting a child for the same behavior is unfair and may cause emotional or behavior problems. Both parents need to decide which behaviors are desirable and which are undesirable.

If you are single-parenting your child, clarify your goals and set realistic expectations for your child's behavior by frequently talking with another adult who also cares for your child. Grandparents or a baby-sitter may be helping to rear your child on a day-to-day basis. If so, be sure that you and the other adult have consistent expectations and goals for your child.

Setting Family Rules

Both you and your spouse need to jointly determine the rules you want your child to follow. When possible, encourage your child to participate when making or modifying rules. If he helps to set a rule, he is more likely to follow it and less likely to resent it. Once a rule is decided, however, you should expect him to follow it. He needs to know which of his behaviors you like and which ones are unacceptable. Of course, never tell your child that he is a "bad child." However, do tell him which behaviors you consider unacceptable.

The Twins Help To Set A Rule

Greg and Adam, four-year-old twins, loved to roughhouse and wrestle with each other. Wrestling in the house was okay when they were two years old and when they were very small. However, they were growing rapidly and the house was taking a beating.

Mother and Father sat down with them and explained that they were "bigger now" and that a new rule was needed. The twins asked, *"Can we wrestle in the family room if we don't do it anyplace else?"* Their parents agreed and a new rule was born: *"No wrestling anywhere in the house — except in the family room."*

Whenever you establish a rule, your children should know the rule well enough to repeat it when asked to do so. Greg and Adam's parents helped the twins to learn the rule by saying it with them. Mother or Father could ask, *"What is the rule about wrestling?"* And either Greg or Adam would respond, *"The rule is — no wrestling anywhere in the house, except in the family room."* Post major rules as helpful reminders for the children.

Giving Effective Instructions And Commands

"Please pick up your toys," is a simple request. *"Stop throwing food!"* or *"Come here and hang up the coat that you threw on the floor!"* are commands.

Parents of children who don't mind are often unable to give clear, emphatic instructions or commands to their children. All parents, especially parents of hard-to-handle children, must be able to give clear, effective instructions or commands. When you use time-out, an especially effective method of discipline, you must be able to tell your child, *"Go to time-out immediately!"*

Learning to give commands doesn't mean that you should start barking orders like a drill sergeant. However, if your child usually doesn't mind and even sasses you when you scold him for not minding, you must be able to give clear, effective commands and to back up your commands.

When are commands given? Give your child a command when you want him to *stop* a specific misbehavior *and* you believe that he might disobey a simple request to stop the misbehavior. Also, give a command when you want your child to *start* a particular behavior *and* you believe your child might disobey a simple request to start the behavior.

How should you give a command? Assume that you come into the living room and find Jennifer, your hard-to-handle seven-year-old, jumping up and down on your new sofa. You should walk right up to her, have a stern facial expression, look her in the eye, and maintain eye contact. Call her name and then give her a clear, direct command in a firm tone of voice. Say, *"Jennifer, jumping on the furniture is against the rule. Get off the sofa!"* You have given her a clear command.

Give clear, explicit commands rather than vague ones. Your child is more likely to mind if you say, *"Come here and start putting those toys on the shelf!"* He is less likely to comply with a vague statement such as, *"Do something with all those toys!"*

Don't ask a question or make an indirect comment when you give a command such as, *"It's not nice to jump on the sofa."* Don't say to Jennifer, *"Why are you jumping on the sofa?"* She just might smile at you and say, *"Because it's lots of fun!"*

Also, *don't give your reasons for a rule while the bad behavior is taking place.* The time to explain reasons for a rule is before your child breaks it or after the bad behavior stops. Do not say to Jennifer while she is still bouncing up and down, *"You shouldn't be jumping on the sofa. It cost a lot of money. We still owe the finance company on it. The springs might come loose. . . ."* However, do say to Jennifer, *"Get off the sofa!"*

After you give your command, Jennifer will probably decide to mind you and get off the sofa. However, let's assume that Jennifer decides to disobey your command. She may decide to test you and see if you have anything with which to back up your command. It's not necessary to severely correct or threaten to correct Jennifer in order to back up your command. This might further complicate an already difficult parent-child problem.

You have a very simple and effective backup for your command. You have "time-out!" Later, in Section Two, we'll discuss how to use time-out in such a confrontation — and without your getting intensely angry. For now, remember the following simple steps for giving effective commands. Memorize and, if necessary, practice these steps.

GIVING EFFECTIVE COMMANDS TO YOUR CHILD

PARENTS' CHECK LIST

_____ Steps to follow:

_____1. Move close to your child.

_____2. Have a stern facial expression.

_____3. Say his or her name.

_____4. Get and maintain eye contact.

_____5. Use a firm tone of voice.

_____6. Give a direct, simple, and clear command.

_____7. Back up your command with time-out, if necessary.

Children Need Discipline And Love

Discipline means teaching a child self-control and improved behavior. Your child learns self-respect and self-control by receiving both love and discipline from you. We discipline our children because we love them and we want them to become responsible, competent adults. Being an effective parent requires love, knowledge, effort, and time. This book will teach you basic principles for changing behavior and practical skills for helping your child. To actually help your child, however, you must repeatedly practice these skills and you must provide effort and time, as well as love.

A WELL-ADJUSTED CHILD

A child who is personally and socially well-adjusted feels good about himself *and* about others. He feels *"I'M OK"* and he feels *"YOU'RE OK."*

A well-adjusted child is both loved and disciplined by his parents. He respects the rights of others and he expects others to respect his rights.

"Reasons" Parents Don't Discipline Their Kids

There are various reasons why some parents avoid disciplining their children. These parents need to be aware of why they are hesitant to discipline and to overcome their resistance to disciplining. You can't expect your child to change her behavior if you are not first willing to change your own behavior. The following are various reasons why parents sometimes find it difficult to change their own behavior.

• **The Hopeless Parent.** This parent feels that her child is unable to change and will always behave poorly. She has given up on her child.

"In And Out Of The Garbage Can"

It was the end of the school day and Mrs. Williams had stopped to talk about her son, Kevin, with his first grade teacher. Whenever possible, Mrs. Williams complained about her son's bad behavior to whomever would listen. However, she never attempted to actually discipline her young son.

While Mrs. Williams and Kevin's teacher were talking, Kevin was down the hall playing near a large open garbage can. Mrs. Williams said, *"I can't do a thing with Kevin. He never does what he is supposed to do."*

As mother and teacher talked, and as they continued to watch Kevin from a distance, Kevin crawled in and out of the large garbage can!

Kevin's teacher said, *"Do you see what Kevin is doing? He is going in and out of that garbage can!"* Mother responded with, *"Yes, he is always doing something like that. Only yesterday, he jumped in a mud puddle and. . . ."*

Never once did Mother give Kevin a command such as, *"Get out of the garbage can!"* She never asked him to stop what he was doing. She never actively helped Kevin to improve his bad behavior. Mother had given up on her young son.

• **The Nonconfronting Parent.** This parent avoids confronting his child. He really doesn't expect his child to mind and his child realizes this. Sometimes this parent fears he will lose his child's love if he makes any demands on him. Hearing "I hate you," "You're a terrible father," or "I wish I had a new Daddy" completely devastates this parent and neutralizes his will to discipline.

"THE LOW ENERGY PARENT"

"Where did he get all of his energy? He certainly didn't get it from me. I feel tired and worn out all the time — especially when I watch him. . . ."

• **The Low Energy Parent.** He or she can't seem to muster the parenting energy necessary to keep up with an active or misbehaving child. Sometimes, a mother or father is a single parent and holds a full-time job. Occasionally, the low energy parent is suffering from a short-term or chronic depression.

• **The Guilty Parent.** This parent blames herself for her child's problems and feels especially guilty when she attempts to discipline her child. Self-blame and guilt prevent her from teaching her son or daughter improved behavior. This parent becomes permissive and passive.

• **The Angry Parent.** Many parents become emotionally upset and angry each time they discipline their child. Since they can't discipline without being angry and upset and feeling miserable as a consequence, they simply ignore their child's misbehavior. The time-out method, however, helps you to be composed when you correct your child.

• **The Hindered Parent.** Sometimes a parent is hindered by a spouse when attempting to discipline their child. If this happens to you, continue talking with your spouse about desirable goals for your child. After agreeing on acceptable goals, work on getting agreement on appropriate methods of discipline. Sometimes relatives or friends interfere when you discipline your child. Frequently the same people who get upset if you do discipline your child, also get upset if you don't discipline your child! Don't let others discourage you from being an effective and self-confident parent.

• **The Troubled Parent.** Marital problems, financial problems, and other difficult life situations sometimes become a heavy burden for a parent. Often, this parent lacks sufficient energy, time, and motivation to help his or her child.

Parenting a child and holding a family together is a difficult and challenging task. Psychologists and other professionals can help parents gain increased understanding of themselves and their family and can help them improve their parenting skills. Chapter 22 tells when and how to get professional help for you or your child

Main Points To Remember:

- Parents must agree about which behaviors are desirable and undesirable.

- Communicate clearly with your child.

- Be able to give clear, effective commands.

- Your child needs your discipline as well as your love. If something is preventing you from disciplining your child, determine what it is and work toward correcting it.

SOS Free Resources!
Over 20 practical resources
audio clips and video clips
for parents & counselors at
www.sosprograms.com

Chapter 3

Ways Of Increasing
Good Behavior

"That's great!   You're learning to tie your own shoes!"

Encouragement, words of praise, and a loving touch strengthen good behavior.

Do you remember teaching a child how to tie his shoes? You first showed him how to do it. Then you asked him to try the first step. When he attempted this new task, you gave him lots of attention and encouragement. He responded by working even harder to please you.

Your encouragement, close attention, smiles, hugs, pats, and words of approval are extremely important to your child and strengthen his behavior. This chapter will show you various methods of rewarding your child in order to get good behavior from him.

Just as it's important to reward your child's good behavior, it's important to *fail to reward bad behavior*. When you see behavior that you don't want your child to continue, one effective option is to actively ignore it.

Use Active Ignoring

ACTIVE IGNORING

"I'll be glad when he stops his temper tantrum. I'm getting bored looking at these flowers. . . ."

Good for mother! She is using active ignoring — withdrawing her attention and herself from her misbehaving child.

Active ignoring is briefly removing all attention from your misbehaving child. Active ignoring is being sure that you don't accidentally reward his bad behavior with attention.* This method of managing children is particularly effective in reducing the tantrums of toddlers and preschoolers. If you scold or pay attention to your child while he is having a tantrum, you might unintentionally reward that behavior. Try active ignoring in order to weaken his tantrum behavior. If your child is in a safe place, walk out of the room and wait until his tantrum ceases before returning. Or, you might turn your back and pretend to be absorbed in something else. When his bad behavior stops, give him lots of attention. Also, be sure that your child's bad behavior

---

*Active ignoring of inappropriate behavior enables you to follow Child Rearing Rule #2, "Don't 'accidentally' reward bad behavior," described in Chapter 1. Not rewarding a particular bad behavior is called *"extinction"* and it weakens that bad behavior.

doesn't push you into giving him a material reward (such as cookies before dinner) or an activity reward (such as watching a late TV movie on a school night).

How do you use active ignoring? Follow the points listed in the table.

Use *Active Ignoring*

For Some Misbehaviors

____ Guidelines to follow:

____ 1. Briefly remove all attention from your child.

____ 2. Refuse to argue, scold, or talk.

____ 3. Turn your head and avoid eye contact.

____ 4. Don't show anger in your manner or gestures.

____ 5. Pretend to be absorbed in some other activity — or leave the room.

____ 6. Be sure your child's bad behavior doesn't get him a material reward or activity reward.

____ 7. Give your child lots of attention when his bad behavior stops.

Use *active ignoring* to weaken these misbehaviors:

• Whining and fussing

• Pouting and sulking

• Loud crying intended to manipulate parents

• Loud complaining

• Continuous begging and demanding

• Breath holding and mild tantrums

Active ignoring often helps to reduce misbehavior. However, when it doesn't, consider using one of the other methods described in this chapter or in succeeding chapters.

Reward Good Alternative Behavior

If your child's undesirable "target behavior" is whining, then the alternative behavior is talking in a normal tone of voice. If your daughter normally whines when she wants something, then you should praise her when she asks for something without whining. *Reward the alternative behavior in order to strengthen it.**

Rewarding Good Alternative Behavior —

Examples For Parents

Target Behavior To Be Decreased (Use active ignoring or mild correction)	*Good* Behavior To Be Increased (Use praise and attention)
1. Whining	1. Talking in a normal tone of voice
2. Toy Grabbing	2. Toy sharing; toy trading
3. Temper tantrums when frustrated	3. Self-control when frustrated
4. Hostile teasing	4. Playing cooperatively
5. Swearing	5. Talking without swearing
6. Hitting	6. Solving problems using words

*Using rewards to increase good behavior which is an alternative to the undesirable target behavior is called "reinforcement of alternative behavior" or "differential reinforcement of other behavior."

Assume that Christopher, your four-year-old, usually has a temper tantrum when he doesn't get what he wants — like when he doesn't get a cookie just before dinner. The next time you turn down one of his requests, be sure to reward him with praise if he demonstrates self- control. Say to him, *"Christopher, you didn't get a cookie this time, but you still behaved yourself. I'm proud of that grown-up behavior. After we eat dinner you may have three cookies!"*

What behavior has to go? What is the behavior you want? Wait for that good behavior. Then *"catch your child being good"* and reward him. If your child doesn't seem to know how to perform the desirable behavior, such as sharing toys or trading toys, teach it to him. Teaching your child the desirable behavior is discussed next.

Help Your Child To Practice Good Behavior

Help your child to practice the behavior that you want her to learn. For example, if your daughter grabs toys away from another child, tell her to trade toys instead. Then demonstrate toy trading yourself and help her to actually practice this skill.

Toy-Grabbing Gloria

When three-year-old Gloria wanted a toy from her baby sister, she often grabbed it. Gloria's parents didn't allow her to keep the toy because that rewarded her for grabbing toys. However, Gloria persisted.

To help his daughter change, Mr. Scott developed a two-part plan. For the first part, Gloria either received a scolding or a time-out when she grabbed a toy.

For the second part, Mr. Scott helped Gloria learn to trade toys. If Gloria wanted a toy truck from her sister, she showed her another toy, and then offered to trade toys. Sometimes Gloria offered four or five different toys before her baby sister agreed to trade.

Mr. Scott taught Gloria the skill of toy trading by first demonstrating this skill himself and by having her watch. He traded toys with the baby. Then Gloria practiced toy trading with the baby and Mr. Scott watched. When Gloria was successful, he praised her efforts. However, when Gloria grabbed a toy from her baby sister, he scolded her or placed her in time-out.

Gloria became good at toy trading and also spent more time sharing toys and playing with her sister. Mr. Scott weakened toy grabbing by using a mild correction. He taught Gloria toy trading to replace toy grabbing.

Use Grandma's Rule

Help your children to do unpleasant tasks by using Grandma's Rule.* *Grandma's Rule states, "After you do your chore, then you get to play."* It's easier to begin and complete an unpleasant task if we get to have fun afterward.

Using Grandma's Rule —

Examples for parents

After you:	*then* you get to:
1. complete your math	1. watch television.
2. wash the supper dishes	2. go out and play ball.
3. straighten your room	3. play video games.
4. take a nap	4. go swimming.
5. eat your brussels sprouts	5. eat dessert.
6. practice the piano for twenty minutes	6. visit a friend.

Don't reverse Grandma's Rule. An example of reversing Grandma's Rule is to say, *"You can watch television now if you promise to do your math homework later tonight."* If your daughter always procrastinates with her math because she hates it, she won't be motivated to finish it by first watching television. She will continue to avoid her math. She will also feel guilty or upset for failing to complete it. Promises to begin a task and guilt don't help children to do unpleasant chores. Having fun afterward is a good motivator.

Getting your child to do something distasteful by reversing Grandma's Rule is difficult to do — like driving your car somewhere in reverse. Use Grandma's Rule correctly.

---

* Grandma's Rule is also called the Premack Principle.

Set a Good Example

Parents constantly demonstrate or "model" behavior which their children observe. Your child learns how to behave and misbehave by observing and imitating your behavior and the behavior of others. Don't unintentionally demonstrate behavior that you wouldn't like to see in your child.

CHILD REARING *MISTAKES* WHICH PARENTS MAKE

You are an *example* for your child!

Model only behavior that is acceptable for your child to imitate.

Your child pays particularly close attention to you when you are frustrated with a problem or having a conflict with another person. *By watching you, she is learning how she might handle her own frustrations and conflicts with others in the future.*

If you use a lot of sarcasm and criticism in dealing with other people, you're actually teaching your child to use sassy talk and complaining as a way of dealing with you and other people. By watching their parents, some kids learn that people swear if they get hurt. Sometimes children learn to have temper tantrums by watching their parents lose control of their own emotions and behavior. *You are a role model for your child whether you want to be or not! Be a good model!*

Children also learn how to behave by watching people on television and in the movies. Many programs show people trying to solve problems and conflicts with others by using aggression and violence. Monitor the kind of television programs and movies your kids watch. Reduce your child's exposure to violent models.

Be An Organized Parent

Be organized and plan ahead to be an effective parent. Anticipate your child's needs before his bad behavior forces you to meet his needs. When you allow your child's bad behavior to force you to meet his needs, you unintentionally reward that bad behavior.

HOUSEHOLD CONFUSION

"Listen, Julie, I'm going to have to get off the phone. The kids are starting to get wild!"

Sometimes the entire family situation becomes disorganized. Often, in such a situation, the *misbehavior* of children rapidly increases. Reorganize the situation as quickly as you can. Being an effective parent takes not only love and discipline, but a lot of time and planning.

If you are shopping with your children, return home before they are completely exhausted. If your children begin to fuss with each other during religious services, don't scold or threaten.

Simply sit between them. The time to have a long telephone conversation is not just before supper when your children are hungry and fussing with each other. If you and your child are spending the evening visiting friends, avoid staying hours past your child's normal bedtime.

Clear family rules, predictable routines, and consistency in daily activities will help your children develop mature behavior. Regular times for waking, healthy snacks, meals, and bedtime will help your child anticipate what is expected of her. And she will be better behaved as a result. Limiting her snacking during the day will encourage her to eat the food offered at meals.

Your children, especially if they are young, need a lot of care and supervision. As parents, we really don't go "off duty" until our children are asleep and even then we are "on call." A favorite time of day for busy mothers and fathers is "after the children are asleep."

Main Points To Remember:

- *Encourage and praise* your child's good behavior.

- *Actively ignore* some misbehaviors.

- After targeting an undesirable behavior, *reward the good alternative behavior.*

- Help your child to *practice behavior* you want him to learn.

- Use *Grandma's Rule* to help your child perform unpleasant chores.

- Be an organized parent. Make clear family rules, predictable routines, and consistency in your child's daily activities.

- *Set a good example* for your child.

ANGER – USED AS AN INSTRUMENT
TO GET WHAT YOU WANT

"Get me a Coke! Get me a Coke NOW!"
(from The SOS Video)

Instrumental anger is the anger a child uses as an instrument or lever, to pressure others to give him what he wants. Unfortunately, some parents give in and accidentally reward their child for using anger, a fit, or emotional upsetness as an instrument for controlling the family and others.

For example, only when Michael expresses increasing anger does mother give in and give him both ice cream and a Coke. Earlier, she had told him *"no dessert"* because he didn't eat his supper.

What is Michael believing and telling himself that causes him to behave aggressively? At a low level of self-awareness, Michael is saying to himself, *"Mother must give me that Coke and if she doesn't, it's awful and I-can't-stand-it! I must have that Coke! I'm going to get real upset, and then she'll give in!"*

Michael has accidentally learned to use emotional upsetness and anger to get what he wants. If this way of thinking and acting becomes a habit, he will be at high risk for experiencing emotional and behavioral problems as an adolescent and adult.

To see a brief video clip of this example (in either English or Spanish) along with solutions parents can implement, go to "Rewarding Bad Behavior" at **www.sosprograms.com**

Chapter 4

What Is Time-Out?
When Do Parents Use It?

A "typical tantrum"

Time-out is especially effective for managing impulsive, hard-to-handle behaviors such as tantrums.

Questions Parents Ask

• *"What is time-out?"*

• *"Could time-out emotionally harm my child?"*

• *"How early can I start using time-out with my toddler?"*

• *"Which of my child's bad behaviors can be decreased by the time-out method?"*

• *"Do other methods of child management work better in certain situations? If so, what are they?"*

Time-Out Before Supper

Mary had a long day at the office, picked up four-year-old Jason from day-care, and now was starting supper. Both Mary and Jason were tired and hungry. *"I want that box of cookies,"* Jason demanded, as he pointed to the open cupboard. Mary replied, *"You may have a glass of milk and two crackers to hold you over. Dinner will be ready in 30 minutes. You may have cookies for dessert. . . ."*

She set milk and crackers in front of Jason. He immediately replied, *"I don't want any dumb milk"* and backhanded the glass of milk, sending it across the table and onto the floor. Feeling extremely angry, she said sternly, *"Time-out! You knocked the glass over. Go now!"* Angry and crying, Jason got down from the table and walked slowly to the time-out place, a utility room at the end of the hall. Mary picked up the small kitchen timer, set it for four minutes, and placed it near the door of the utility room. She then returned to the kitchen.

After four minutes the timer rang. Jason appeared in the kitchen, picked up the two crackers on the table, and turned on the kitchen TV. Looking up at his mother a few minutes later, he said. *"Guess what, Mom, the Roberts got a new puppy. . . ."*

Following Mary's use of time-out, the mother-son relationship quickly returned to normal. Mary kept her "cool" and also quickly dealt with the demanding tantrum behavior of her son.

JASON

"I don't want any dumb milk!"

What Is Time-Out?

In basketball and football, "time-out" is a brief interruption or suspension of play for participants. As a method of discipline, "time-out" is a brief interruption of activities for your child.

Time-out is placing a child in a dull, boring place immediately following bad behavior. He stays there until a timer signals that he can leave. He stays in time-out one minute for each year of age.

Time-out means time-out from rewards, reinforcement, attention, and interesting activities for the child. You quickly remove your child from the reinforcing or pleasurable situation in which the misbehavior occurs and briefly place her in a quiet, boring area which is not reinforcing or enjoyable at all. By placing your child in time-out, you prevent her from getting attention or other rewards following her undesirable behavior.*

Advantages Of Using The Time-Out Method

- Time-out quickly weakens many types of bad behaviors.

- Time-out helps stop some kinds of misbehavior permanently. Improved behaviors then take their place.

- It's easy for parents to learn and use.

- Parents report feeling less angry and upset because they have an effective plan.

- Parents are a rational and nonaggressive model for their children.

- The parent-child relationship quickly returns to normal following the use of time-out.

The time-out method of discipline has two goals. The immediate goal is to bring a quick stop to the problem behavior. The long-term goal is to help your child achieve self-discipline.

---

*Time-out is a method of nonreinforcement for undesirable behavior as well as a mild correction. Time-out is an effective method for following Child Rearing Rule #2, "Don't accidentally reward bad behavior" and Rule #3, "Correct some bad behavior," described in Chapter 1.

Time-Out From Your Child's Point Of View

SAMMIE

"I'd Rather Get A Spanking!"

Mr. Gordon used the time-out method for several months and was successful in reducing hitting and pushing by his five-year-old son, Sammie. Mr. Gordon greatly decreased his use of swats, spankings, and intense scoldings. He was interested in his son's feelings regarding time-out compared with more aggressive forms of discipline.

On a quiet Saturday afternoon, Mr. Gordon causally asked, *"Sammie, when you hit your little brother, what should Dad do? Spank you or put you in time-out?"* Sammie replied, *"I'd rather get a spanking! I want to get it over with. There is nothing to do in time-out. I don't like time-out!"*

The time-out method is effective in correcting bad behavior because kids hate being in time-out. Many children prefer to get a spanking or a severe scolding rather than briefly being placed in time-out.

Children don't like time-out because they experience a number of immediate losses even though these losses are brief and mild. When placed in time-out, kids lose attention from their family. They lose power and control and the ability to anger and upset their parents. Kids lose the freedom to play with toys and games and to join interesting activities. Since the time-out method is swift and definite, kids are less able to avoid this form of discipline. Your child will usually be irritated with you *when* sent to time-out and *during* time-out. Ordinarily, your child's annoyance will rapidly disappear after time-out is over.

Both children and adults resist changing their behavior. Kids don't want to stop their troublesome behavior. However, if they continue with these problem behaviors, they receive repeated time-outs. Consequently, they find these problem behaviors easier to give up! Kids then explore different ways to meet their needs. When these new behaviors are rewarded, they are strengthened and more likely to occur in the future. Time-out weakens your child's old problem behaviors and encourages new acceptable behavior to emerge.

Time-Out Won't Emotionally Harm Your Child

Time-out, when correctly used, is safe and effective in stopping your child's bad behavior. It helps children to grow out of emotional problems. There is no evidence that time-out, correctly used, emotionally harms children. In the audio program (on CD and audiotape), *How To Use Time-Out Effectively*, Todd (age nine) and Lisa (age eleven) describe their personal feelings and reactions regarding time-out.* Many parents report that listening to these children has reduced their concerns about time-out. Listen to these interviews yourself!

Parents, however, often make various time-out mistakes. Chapter 6 describes the exact steps for correctly using time-out.

Your Child Between Two And Twelve

You can successfully use the time-out method if your child is between two and twelve years of age. However, when you *begin* using time-out with your child, he shouldn't be older than eleven. For the older child, use other methods of child management discussed in this book.

Observe The Bad Behavior Yourself

Ideally, you should *see or hear* the bad behavior so that you may immediately send your child to time-out. To be most effective, place your child in time-out within 10 seconds after the bad behavior. Immediacy of time-out is especially important if your child is between two and four years old.

---

*Listen to these interviews at www.sosprograms Order the complete *How To Use Time-Out Effectively* audio program from SOS Programs & Parents Press.

Bad behavior repeats itself! If you just missed an opportunity to time-out a bad behavior, be patient. Another misbehavior is likely to occur soon!

Which Kinds Of Misbehavior Deserve Time-Out?

Time-out is effective in helping to correct your child's persistent misbehaviors that are impulsive, aggressive, emotional, or hostile. When time-out is compared with other methods of discipline, *it is one of the most effective methods available for eliminating both severe and mild problem behaviors.* However, recognize that time-out is not the only method of discipline which can reduce the following Category A behaviors.

Category A Behaviors —
Misbehavior That Deserves Time-Out

Hitting
Temper Tantrums
Hostile teasing of other children; provoking others
Sassy talk or back-talk to parents and other adults
Angry screaming and screeching
Toy grabbing from another child
Toy throwing
Destroying toys
Kicking others
Biting or threatening to bite
Hair pulling
Choking others
Spitting or threatening to spit at others
Throwing dirt, rocks or sticks at others
Mistreating or hurting pets and other animals
Obnoxious loud crying "intended" to punish parents
Slapping
Pinching
Scratching

Tattling
Doing dangerous things such as riding a tricycle into the street
Whining loudly
Hitting others with an object
Threatening by word or gesture to hit or hurt others
Cursing and swearing
Pushing others standing on a stairway
Food throwing at the dinner table
Purposefully damaging furniture or the house
Mocking or trying to humiliate parents
Loud complaining or demanding behavior, after a warning
Name calling and "making faces" at others
Persistently interrupting adult conversation, after a warning
Disobeying a "command" to immediately *stop* a particular misbehavior

In looking over this shopping list of 33 bad behaviors, do you recognize any of your child's behavior which you wish to eliminate? Parents who have used the time-out method have been able to reduce or eliminate each misbehavior in Category A. Whether or not you consider a behavior bad or bad enough to deserve time-out, depends upon your values and upon the goals which you and your spouse have for your child.

However, time-out is not the solution for all problem behavior of children. Time-out should *not* be used for Category B behavior problems.

Category B Behaviors
Do *Not* Use Time-Out On These Problem Behaviors

Pouting, sulking
Irritableness, bad moods, grumpiness
Failing or forgetting to do chores
Failing to pick up clothes and toys
Not doing homework or piano practice
Overactive behavior (but *do* time-out aggressive or destructive acts)
Fearfulness
Being dependent, timid or passive
Seclusiveness, wanting to be alone
Behaviors *not* observed by the parent

Use other forms of child management to help with these problem behaviors. Time-out is *not* effective when used on Category B behavior. *Actively ignore* quiet pouting, soft crying, and whimpering (Chapter 3).

Parents often ask if they can use time-out to get their child to *start* doing something which is fairly complex such as, *"Straighten your room"* or *"Do your homework."* Time-out is effective in *stopping bad behavior.* Threatening your child with time-out doesn't encourage him to *begin* a chore which is both complex and distasteful. *Time-out is a behavior stopper and not a behavior starter.* To get your child to do a distasteful chore, consider using *Grandma's Rule* (Chapter 5), *token rewards* (Chapter 14), or, for the older child, a *parent-child contract* (Chapter 14).

When you press your child to do a disagreeable chore, she might sass you or have a temper tantrum. Do use time-out on this back-talk or temper tantrum. Once you stop this interfering behavior, it will be easier to get your child to do distasteful chores. Be sure to praise her efforts to begin and complete unpleasant tasks.

Select Only One Or Two Target Behaviors

You and your spouse need to select one or two behaviors on which to begin the time-out method. These behaviors are called *target behaviors because your aim or goal is to change them.* Use time-out *consistently and repeatedly* on these target behaviors.

Don't *begin* using time-out on all of your child's inappropriate or unacceptable behaviors. He might spend all day in time-out! After gaining success in decreasing the first target behavior, you can select another target behavior to be decreased.

How do you go about selecting a target behavior? Look over the list of Category A misbehaviors and choose one of these or a similar misbehavior. The behavior should be countable. For example, be able to actually count the number of times that your child sasses you or tattles on a brother or sister.

Also, be sure that the target behavior you select occurs frequently. You won't be able to obtain adequate experience in learning how to use time-out unless the behavior occurs at least once a day.

SELECT A TARGET BEHAVIOR
AND
USE TIME-OUT REPEATEDLY ON THE TARGET BEHAVIOR

"Darn! Busted again! I've got to stop teasing my brother. I land in time-out every time. I'm going to find something else interesting to do besides teasing him. Maybe I'll play my CD's or visit a friend. . . ."

Time-out is effective because it stops bad behavior ("*teasing my brother*") and thus allows improved good behavior (*"I'll play my CD's or visit a friend."*) to emerge. Do use time-out repeatedly to stop the selected target behavior. When the improved good behavior emerges, reward it.

When first beginning the time-out method you might select two target behaviors, one minor problem behavior and one major problem behavior. Begin using time-out with a minor target behavior such as tattling or teasing. These are easy target behaviors to handle because children are usually not extremely emotional or angry when tattling or teasing.

Later, after getting experience in using time-out, move on to a major target behavior such as hitting or temper tantrums. These misbehaviors are usually more challenging since children are more emotional or angry when demonstrating these behaviors.

Use time-out repeatedly on the target behavior. When first using time-out, use it each time the target behavior occurs. You should see a 50- to 90-percent decrease in the target behavior within one or two weeks.

Count How Often The Target Behavior Occurs

Before you begin using time-out, it's a good idea to actually count and record how often the target behavior occurs. Then, after you have been using time-out for a while, you can see how much the misbehavior has decreased.

Some parents place tally marks on a wall calendar, a convenient place to keep a record of the target behavior. For example, one mother put a mark on the calendar each time her daughter tattled. Mother didn't bother keeping track of "tattles" all day long — just the tattles which occurred each day from supper-time to bedtime.

A curious thing sometimes occurs if a child see his parent recording tally marks. Often the child's target behavior abruptly decreases without the parent even using time-out.

You may think it's a nuisance to keep a record of target behavior. However, this record will tell you how effective you have been in reducing your child's misbehavior.

Main Points To Remember:

- *Time-out means time-out from rewards, reinforcement, attention, and interesting activities for the child.*

- Time-out, correctly used, won't emotionally harm your child.

- Select one or two *undesirable target behaviors* to be decreased.

- Use time-out *immediately* and *repeatedly* after the target behavior occurs.

- Follow the *steps for using time-out* which are described in Chapters 6 through 11.

Chapter 5

Major Methods For Stopping Bad Behavior

How would *you* handle this situation?

Questions Parents Ask About Correction

- *"Should I use mild correction to change my child's misbehavior?"*

- *"What kinds of mild correction are effective in reducing misbehavior?"*

- *"Can the use of correction be emotionally harmful to my child?"*

- *"Why do my children continue to misbehave after they are corrected?"*

There are five different types of mild correction that you can use to help your child. One of these methods, time-out, is brief and is especially effective in stopping persistent misbehavior that is impulsive, explosive, and hard to handle.

Other chapters in this book describe, step by step, when and how to use the time-out method. However, time-out does have a limitation. When you use time-out, you should use it *immediately* after the bad behavior occurs. What do you do about serious misbehavior which you discover minutes or hours later?

Four other methods of mild correction are effective even if you can't apply them immediately. They are: (1) *scolding and disapproval,* (2) *natural consequences,* (3) *logical consequences,* and (4) *behavior penalty.* This chapter describes these methods and how you can correctly use them.

To be a confident and competent parent, know and use various methods to manage your child's problem behaviors. You can easily learn these effective methods! It's a lot easier to deal with a particular misbehavior if you know several ways to correctly handle it.

Mild correction can stop or weaken your child's bad behavior. However, it can't increase good behavior when used alone. As emphasized in earlier chapters, you also must frequently *reward good behavior.*

Correctly Using Mild Correction

_____   Guidelines to follow:

_____   1. Use correction sparingly.

_____   2. Use mild correction only.

_____   3. Correct quickly after the bad behavior occurs.

_____   4. Correct when you are in control of yourself.

_____   5. Briefly state a reason for the correction.

_____   6. Avoid physical correction.

Correction is an unpleasant consequence or penalty that follows a behavior. When you use mild correction, be sure to observe the correct guidelines.

The correct use of *mild* correction won't emotionally harm your child. Often it is essential for improving her behavior. However, severe correction, sarcasm, and grim threats can hurt her self-esteem and emotional well-being. Children who are severely corrected may become extremely withdrawn or may act more aggressive and belligerent toward others. Mothers and fathers who severely discipline their children frequently carry a heavy burden of guilt.

PROBLEMS PARENTS FACE

"My sister told me to do it. It's not my fault. . . . Let's just forget about correction this time. . . ."

Being A Rational And Nonaggressive Model

When at their wits' end, parents often try to correct or control their kids by making irrational threats such as, *"You're grounded all summer for doing that!"* or *"I'm going to pull every hair from your head unless you. . . !"* Parents who use severe or frequent spankings as a method of discipline often don't realize that several different methods of *mild correction* can be more effective in changing behavior.

Remember, your child will imitate your behavior. If you shout, make irrational threats, or spank, you are "modeling" this behavior for your daughter to imitate. She may yell, become emotionally upset, or attempt to "manage" others physically. When using time-out discipline, you are a rational and nonaggressive role model for your child.

Your job as a parent is often stressful and upsetting. Sometimes your child may intentionally try to anger you. Children enjoy getting attention and controlling their parents by making them angry and overly emotional. However, you can resist yielding to your anger. You can do it! You can avoid yelling and screaming, making grim threats, using sarcasm, giving harsh spankings, or using other forms of severe or ineffective correction. Lets look at the following methods of discipline.

DISCIPLINE *MISTAKES* WHICH PARENTS MAKE

"This will teach you   "This will teach you!"
to behave!"

Children imitate the behavior of their parents. By using spankings and threats, you teach your daughter to use aggressive methods to "manage" others.

Using Scolding And Disapproval Correctly

The Missing Cookies

Mother had just discovered that seven-year-old Michelle had disobeyed her and eaten most of the chocolate chip cookies being saved for dessert. She walked toward her daughter and in a stern voice said, *"Michelle, I'm very disappointed that you ate the cookies. I was saving them for supper. Now we won't have enough for dessert tonight."*

Michelle's mother is correctly using disapproval, a form of mild correction commonly used by parents. When you are scolding for bad behavior, move close to your child, look her in the eye, be stern, express your feelings, and name the undesirable behavior. It's important to maintain self-control and to avoid making sarcastic or belittling remarks.

Be brief and calm when scolding your child. Some children enjoy a lengthy tongue-lashing and watching their parent become upset. They like getting the extra attention from their mother or father, even if that attention is negative.

PROBLEMS PARENTS FACE

Scolding Back!

A scolding *doesn't* help some children to improve their behavior. They merely argue or scold back.

Avoid "nattering" at your child when you want her to improve her behavior. *Nattering is a combination of nagging, chattering, scolding, and complaining.* For example, mother might have said to Michelle, *"I'm mad that you ate all the cookies that I was saving for dessert. Another thing, your hair is a mess again and you left all your toys in the living room. You never appreciate what I do for you. Furthermore, . . ."* Nattering doesn't help your child to improve her behavior, and it weakens your relationship. Don't natter at your child!

Remember to show disapproval of your child's behavior and not of your child. Don't criticize her personality or character. Let her know that you still respect and love her as a person. Instead of saying, *"You are a mean girl for hitting your brother,"* say *"It was mean to hit your brother."* Don't say *"You are a naughty girl."* Do say *"That was a naughty thing to do."* When you scold, be sure to disapprove of your child's behavior and not of your child.

An effective time to use disapproval is just as your child's misbehavior is getting started. For example, your two children may begin with playful teasing and then rapidly move on to hostile teasing. When you find this happening, quickly express disapproval. You might say, *"I really don't like the teasing that's going on between the two of you. I don't mind a little playful teasing, but when it continues, you two frequently get into an argument. I don't want to hear any more teasing this evening!"*
For many children, disapproval is normally sufficient when used alone as a mild correction. However, if your child usually becomes angry or argues when you scold him, then scolding isn't very effective. When scolding and disapproval are not effective, consider using time-out or another form of mild correction.

Signs that scolding and disapproval are *not* effective with your child

- Your child usually scolds back, sasses, mocks, or argues with you.

- Your child smiles, ignores you, or seems inattentive.

- He has a temper tantrum when scolded.

- He seems to enjoy getting the extra attention from you, even though it's negative attention.

Natural Consequences For Bad Behavior

PROBLEMS PARENTS FACE

"Let's see. . . . Should I use TIME-OUT or should I let Kitty give NATURAL CONSEQUENCES?"

A natural consequence for not wearing gloves on a cold day is having cold hands. Staying after school or losing recess is a natural consequence for not doing a homework assignment.

A natural consequence is an event that normally or naturally happens to a child following his bad behavior, unless you step in to prevent the consequence. Nature or the "natural order of the world" does the correcting rather than the parent. You allow your child to experience the natural consequences of his own behavior unless there is some danger to his safety.

If six-year-old James teases a friend, his friend may get angry and go home. James will be left without a playmate. Being alone is a natural consequence of teasing one's friend. Consider the various examples of natural consequences for bad behavior described in the box, "Allowing *Natural Consequences* To Occur For Bad Behavior."

Parents who use natural consequences believe that children learn to improve their behavior when they are allowed to experience naturally occurring consequences for their own decisions and actions. Since correction is delivered by nature and not by parents, children are much less likely to get angry at their parents for being corrected.

Allowing *Natural Consequences*

To Occur For Bad Behavior —

Examples For Parents

Bad Behavior	*Natural Consequences*
1. Handling a cat roughly.	1. Getting scratched.
2. Breaking a toy on purpose.	2. Having a broken toy which is not replaced.
3. Teasing neighborhood children.	3. Being avoided by neighborhood children.
4. Not doing a homework assignment.	4. Staying after school the next day if required by the teacher.
5. Not wearing gloves on a cold day.	5. Having cold hands.
6. Not combing your hair.	6. Being told by other children that your hair is a mess.
7. Getting ready for school very slowly in the morning.	7. Being late for school and explaining to the teacher why you are late.
8. Pushing and shoving other children of the same age.	8. Getting pushed and shoved back.
9. Carelessly spilling a drink.	9. Not getting a refill.

Logical Consequences
For Bad Behavior

Applying Logical Consequences
For Bad Behavior —
Examples For Parents

Bad Behavior	*Logical Consequences*
1. Riding a tricycle into the street.	1. Tricycle is put up for one week.
2. Chewing gum gets stuck to furniture, clothes, or hair.	2. No more gum for five days.
3. Swearing on the telephone.	3. Can't phone out for three days.
4. Mistreating or refusal to care for one's pet.	4. Placing the pet in another home, after several warnings and discussions.
5. Refusal to brush teeth regularly.	5. No more candy or soft drinks until regular tooth brushing is begun.
6. Brother and sister argue and fuss all morning.	6. Family outing to a park is cancelled that afternoon.
7. Not eating vegetables at dinner.	7. No dessert.

Sometimes you can't allow natural consequences to occur because it's dangerous for your child. For example, father can't allow three-year-old John to experience *natural consequences* for riding a tricycle into the street. However, father can apply *logical consequences*. If John rides his tricycle in an unsafe place, then he loses the privilege of riding his tricycle for a time. Father can quickly remove the tricycle and not allow John to use it for one week.

When using *logical consequences* to handle problem behavior, *you provide correction for the bad behavior.* Also, you need to make sure that *the correction logically fits the nature of the misbehavior. The correction is a logical or sensible consequence considering the particular bad behavior.* When your child sees a clear and reasonable relationship between her bad behavior and the correction, she is more likely to change her behavior. In addition, she is less likely to resent the correction.

When you apply a logical consequence, it is important to avoid a consequence which is too severe or lasts too long. For example, the consequence of *"No tricycle for two months!"* is too harsh for a three-year-old who rides his tricycle into the street. When angry or emotionally upset by your child's misbehavior, you might declare a consequence that is too extreme. If you make this common mistake, there is a simple solution! Merely tell your child that you made the consequence too severe, and that you have reduced the consequence.

What is the difference between natural consequences and logical consequences? You *allow* natural consequences to occur (your child carelessly breaks a toy and now has a broken toy). You *apply* logical consequences (after your child rides a tricycle into the street you put up the tricycle).

Using Behavior Penalty For Bad Behavior

If you can't think of a logical consequence for a particular misbehavior, then consider using behavior penalty. Behavior penalty is another method of correction which is effective, but mild. *You apply some penalty* (such as no television for one day) *following some specific bad behavior* (such as lying to you).* However,

---

*Behavior penalty is also called "response cost" because a child's undesirable response costs her some penalty.

the penalty is not "logically" related to the particular bad behavior. The penalty consists of a loss of certain privileges, a fine, or an extra chore that your child finds especially distasteful. For example, each time that nine-year-old Heather mistreats her puppy, she loses the privilege of playing her stereo for the rest of that day. The temporary loss of her stereo (the penalty) is not logically related to mistreating her puppy (the behavior). In selecting an effective penalty, Heather's parents need to know what kind of penalty is most meaningful for Heather. *"No bike riding for two days!"* is an ineffective penalty if Heather rarely rides her bike anyway.

Using *Behavior Penalty*

For Bad Behavior —

Examples For Parents

"Kids don't like it when I tattle."
"Kids don't like it when I tattle."
"Kids don't like it when I ...."

Behavior	Penalty
1. Tattling on other children.	1. Having to immediately write three times, *"Kids don't like it when I tattle."*
2. Swearing.	2. A 25 cent fine for each swear word.
3. Lying to parents.	3. No television for one day.
4. Fighting with neighborhood children.	4. No bike riding for two days.
5. Persistent teasing of little brother.	5. Stereo and CDs are "put up" for one day.
6. Failure to clean up one's bedroom by 5:00 p.m.	6. No playing outdoors that evening.

When you use behavior penalty, try to state the penalty before the specific bad behavior occurs. For example, Heather's mother might say, *"Heather, your father and I have talked about the way you mistreat your puppy. In the future when you mistreat Scottie, you'll lose the use of your stereo for the rest of the day."* Mother should have Heather state out loud the misbehavior and the behavior penalty. This will help her to remember to be kind to Scottie.

The box, "Using *Behavior Penalty* For Bad Behavior," gives examples of parents using this method of mild correction.

In situations where it is not practical to use natural consequences or logical consequences to handle misbehavior, consider using behavior penalty. Avoid making the penalty too severe or too lengthy, however.

The box, "Methods Of Mild Correction," provides a brief comparison of the five methods of mild correction discussed in this chapter. These five methods are the most effective forms of mild correction that you can use. To be successful in handling different types of misbehavior, you should know how to use all five methods.

Time-out is extremely effective, but it should be used only with children between the ages of two and twelve. Also, you should apply time-out immediately after the bad behavior occurs. Many parents admit that the most difficult behaviors to handle frequently occur right under their noses. Time-out is particularly helpful in stopping these persistent misbehaviors.

The other methods of mild correction may be used with children who fall within a wide range of ages. These other methods are also most effective if applied as quickly as possible after the misbehavior occurs. However, these methods are still rather effective if applied minutes or a few hours after the misbehavior is discovered.

Avoid expressing intense anger when you use correction. Your child should believe that she got corrected because she behaved badly and not because you got angry.

Bad Behavior Sometimes Persists

Often, children will persist in bad behavior. There are various reasons for this. The amount of reward the child receives for the bad behavior may far outweigh the correction. Nicole may tattle on her brother and enjoy getting him into trouble even though mother shows disapproval for her tattling. In this case,

Methods Of *Mild* Correction — Comparison For Parents

Method of Mild Correction	Age of Child	Effectiveness of Correction	Type of Behaviors Corrected	How Quickly Applied
Time-Out	Two through twelve	Extremely effective	Most behavior, especially hard-to-handle behavior	Immediately, if possible
Scolding and Disapproval	All Ages	Moderately effective	All Behavior	Immediately or later
Natural Consequences	All Ages	Effective	Some Behavior	Immediately or later
Logical Consequences *"I'm putting your crayons up for ONE WEEK!"*	Three through Adolescence	Effective	Most Behavior	Immediately or later
Behavior Penalty For example, *"No TV for rest of the day."* or *"No bike riding for rest of the day."*	Five through Adolescence	Effective	All Behavior	Immediately or later

Nicole's reward (getting her brother into trouble) outweighs her correction (receiving disapproval).

Perhaps a child has learned that he runs very little risk of actually being corrected. For instance, Aaron may occasionally raid the cookie jar, but rarely get caught. If he is caught, his parents may only threaten to correct, but never follow through with actual correction.

Sometimes parents demonstrate a particular behavior themselves — such as swearing — for which they correct their child. Children tend to imitate their parents' behavior even if their parents correct them for that behavior.

As a parent, be consistent in the behavior that you reward and the behavior that you correct. When you do correct, use correction that is both mild and effective.

Main Points To Remember:

- Rewarding good behavior is the easiest and best way to produce desirable behavior.

- Mild correction helps stop your child's bad behavior.

- Use correction sparingly and use mild correction only.

- Be a rational and nonaggressive model when you use correction.

- The most effective methods of mild correction are *time- out, scolding and disapproval, natural consequences, logical consequences, and behavior penalty.*

Section Two

BASIC SKILLS
OF THE TIME-OUT METHOD

Time-out is a powerful method for stopping bad behavior. In this section, you'll learn basic skills for correctly using time-out. Each chapter describes separate steps of the *Time-Out And 10-10 Method*. If you have questions or problems regarding a particular time-out step, you can review the chapter describing that step.

These chapters have separate time-out instructions for managing very young children who are two to four years old, and for older children who are five to twelve years old.

Since parents ask many questions about the correct use of time-out, I have included many examples and illustrations. These chapters summarize and repeat important points. The last chapter tells you how to avoid *Nine Common Time-Out Mistakes*. This chapter also gives you solutions if you think your child might not cooperate with the time-out method.

Let's get started with the time-out method!

See a free video clip at www.sosprograms.com entitled "Time-Out, Effective Use." I describe time-out and time-out is demonstrated with five children.

Listen to "How To Use Time-Out Effectively" audio program. It illustrates and teaches time-out skills. I demonstrate time-out with a two-year old child. Two children, Todd and Lisa, describe their feelings and reactions regarding time-out.

Many parents hesitate to use time-out because they fear that it might be emotionally damaging to their child. Listening to Todd and Lisa talk about time-out will reduce any concerns that you have. This enjoyable audio program is suitable for individual listening or parent workshops.

Listen to Todd and Lisa
tell about time-out!

Go to <www.sosprograms.com> and listen to free audio interviews with Todd and Lisa. They have experienced time-out since age two. Learn how they feel about time-out.

By listening to these interviews you can be a more effective parent by understanding time-out from your child's point of view.

Interview with Todd,
age nine ©

Interview with Lisa,
age eleven ©

Lisa, age eleven, is interviewed by me. Lisa describes her feelings about time-out, how she attempts to rebel against time-out, how her parents handle her rebellious behavior, and if she will use time-out when she has children. This audio interview is both moving and humorous. The interviews along with complete instructions for using time-out are available on CD from SOS Programs & Parents Press. Use the Order Form at the end of this book.

These are the only interviews of which I am aware that describe time-out from your child's point of view. Listen to Todd and Lisa at <www.sosprograms.com>

Also, see free video clips at www.sosprograms.com entitled "Time-Out, Effective Use." I describe time-out and the correct use of time-out is demonstrated with five children.

Download a free copy of "SOS Time-Out Guidelines" at <www.sosprograms.com> These guidelines also tell you how to avoid making nine common time-out mistakes.

Chapter 6

Getting Started With Time-Out

"We have our timer. Let's see what's next. . . ."

Getting started with the time-out method is easy.

You can do it! You can help your child to improve his behavior. Using the time-out method, you and your spouse can be more effective and self-confident parents.

This chapter outlines the time-out method and tells you the basic steps to follow in correctly using time-out for the first time. Other chapters of this book will simplify each of these steps.

Immediately place your child in time-out after he demonstrates the undesirable target behavior — such as hitting or sassy talk. Send him there using no more than *10 words and 10 seconds*. He stays one minute in time-out for each year of age.

Remember! *10 words or less, 10 seconds or less in getting there, and one minute in time-out for each year of age.* By using the *Time-Out And 10-10 Method*, you can be consistent, fair, and effective in helping your child to learn acceptable behavior.

Set a timer for the same number of minutes each time that you place your child in time-out. *Always use a small portable timer that rings.* If you don't have a portable timer now, put one on your shopping list today! You can get one at most hardware and department stores.   The timer keeps accurate track of the time and signals your child when he may leave time-out. *Not using a portable timer is one of the most common mistakes parents make.* Chapter 10 gives many reasons why a portable timer is necessary.

The steps of the time-out method and the number of minutes in time-out are always the same, no matter what your child did. In addition to being effective in changing bad behavior, time-out is easy to use. In fact, unlike other methods of discipline, you will find that time-out gets easier and easier as you use it.

PROBLEMS PARENTS FACE

"I'm not through coloring yet, DUMB-DUMB!"

Handling sassy talk and back-talk is a common problem parents face.

The example of Cindy shows how one mother began using time-out to greatly reduce her daughter's persistent "sassy talk."

"Time-Out For Sassy Talk"

Cindy was an attractive five-year-old with blue eyes and long blonde hair. She was bright, assertive, verbal with adults and children, and generally lovable.

However, Cindy had one bad habit. Cindy was sassy. Cindy was sassy whenever she felt like it. She usually felt like being sassy whenever someone tried to make her do something she didn't want to do. Or stop her from doing something she wanted to do. She was sassy with her parents, her grandparents, relatives, and with other children. Even the babysitter complained to Cindy's parents.

Five-year-old Cindy controlled her parents by talking sassy to them. She made them feel helpless and angry. And when others were present, her parents felt embarrassed. When Mr. and Mrs. Miller scolded Cindy for being sassy, she increased her sassy talk. Her behavior was getting worse.

Mr. and Mrs. Miller had heard about the time-out method of discipline and decided to use this method to help their daughter. Sassy talk was the "target" behavior. They were in their fourth day of using time-out, and Cindy already had been placed in time-out eight times.

Cindy's mother was busy cooking and was getting ready to set the table for supper. Cindy was busy coloring on the same table. Carrying a stack of plates, mother said, *"Please pick up your crayons and coloring books so I can set the table."* Cindy ignored her mother's request and continued coloring. Again her mother stated, *"Cindy, pick up your crayons and books, and do it now!"* Cindy responded, *"I'm not through coloring yet, DUMB-DUMB!"* Cindy's mother immediately said, *"Time-out! That was sassy. Time-out in the bathroom."* Pouting, Cindy got down from the table and marched off to the bathroom. Cindy's mother picked up the portable timer, set it for five minutes, and placed it outside the bathroom door.

Five minutes later the timer rang. When Cindy came into the kitchen, Mrs. Miller said, *"Cindy, why did you have to go to time-out?"* Cindy replied, *"I talked sassy to you."* Mother responded, *"Yes, talking sassy put you in time-out."* Mother then continued setting the table. Good for Cindy's mother! She effectively followed the basic steps of the time-out method. After the target behavior (sassy talk) occurred, she swiftly placed her daughter in time-out, set the timer for five minutes, and put it near the time-out place. She didn't spank, scold, or yell at Cindy. Instead, she simply placed Cindy in time-out. As a consequence of her sassy talk, Cindy experienced a number of immediate, but brief losses. She lost the use of her crayons and her mother's attention. She also lost the ability to control her mother by talking sassy to her.

In the coming weeks, and with the repeated use of time-out, Cindy greatly decreased her sassy talk. She found improved ways of talking to her mother and to other adults.

Basic Steps For *Initially* Using Time-Out — Parents' Check List

_____ **Steps To Follow:**

A portable timer is essential for effective time-out!

___ 1. Select one target behavior on which to use time-out. (Chapter 4)

___* 2. Count how often this target behavior occurs. (Chapter 4)

___ 3. Pick out a boring place for time-out. (Chapter 7)

___ 4. Explain time-out to your child. (Chapter 8)

___ 5. Wait patiently for the target behavior to occur. (Chapter 9)

TARGET BEHAVIOR OCCURS!

___ 6. Place your child in the time-out place and use no more than 10 words and 10 seconds. (Chapter 9)

___ 7. Get the portable timer, set it to ring one minute for each year of age, and place it within hearing distance of your child. (Chapter 10)

___ 8. Wait for the timer to ring — remove all attention from your child while she waits for the timer to ring. (Chapter 10)

___*9. Ask your child, after the timer rings, why she was sent to time-out. (Chapter 11)

*These two steps are important but not essential.

Before you begin the time-out method, be sure you frequently reward your child's good behavior. Also, avoid unintentionally rewarding the behavior on which you plan to use time-out.

In Chapter 4, you learned how to select a target behavior on which to use time-out. Use time-out on this target behavior each time it occurs and not just when you are angry. There should be a major reduction in this target behavior within one or two weeks if you correctly follow the basic steps for using time-out.

Don't start using time-out, until after you have read Chapters 7 through 11. These chapters describe each step of the time-out method and give examples. Also, the instructions in these chapters are tailored for the age of your child.

It's a good idea to look at Chapter 12 before you use time-out for the first time. This chapter discusses Common Time-Out Mistakes And Problems that parents sometimes encounter using time-out.

Main Points To Remember:

- Use the *Time-Out And 10-10 Method*. Send your child to time-out using no more than 10 words and 10 seconds.

- Time-out lasts one minute for each year of your child's age.

- Always use a portable timer that rings.

- Follow the "Basic Steps For Using Time-Out."

How To Use Time-Out Effectively
Audio Program by Lynn Clark, PhD

How To Use Time-Out Effectively audio CD program demonstrates and teaches time-out skills. You'll learn how to avoid 9 common time-out mistakes. I demonstrate time-out with a two year-old child. Todd (age nine) and Lisa (age eleven) describe their feelings and reactions regarding time-out.

You might hesitate to use time-out because you fear that it could be emotionally damaging to your child. Listening to Todd and Lisa will reduce your concerns and answer your questions about time-out.

This audio program is enjoyable and suitable for individual listening. It is especially helpful to counselors who offer parent workshops or parent counseling. Parts of the interviews with the children are humorous. A brief Time-Out Guide, Time-Out Chart, and CD are included in this audio program. Use the Order Form at the end of this book.

Audio Program Content (67 minutes)
by Lynn Clark, PhD

- Introduction

- Basic Child Rearing Rules

- Basic Steps For *Initially* Using Time-Out

- Demonstration of Time-Out With Todd, Age Two

- Interview With Todd, Age Nine
  (listen to at www.sosprograms.com)

- Time-out Mistakes Parents Make

- Interview With Lisa, Age Eleven
  (listen to at www.sosprograms.com)

- Time-Out Questions Parents Ask

- Time-Out For Two

- Time-Out For Toys That Misbehave

- Concluding Comments

Audio CD Program

- CD Audio Disc
  (67 minutes)

- Time-Out Guide

- Illustrated Time-Out Chart

- Additional free resources at www.sosprograms.com

Chapter 7

Picking A Boring Place For Time-Out

"I'll bet my sister is out there having fun. . . ."

The bathroom is a good place for time-out for children five to twelve years old.

An ideal spot for time-out is a dull place or room where your child won't receive any attention from you or other family members. Your child should be able to get there quickly, preferably within 10 seconds.

Where is the best place in your home for time-out? Look over the rooms and areas in your home and choose a safe place which is boring for a child — a place where there is nothing interesting to see or do.

The place you select depends on your child's age. *A time-out chair is best for a child between two and four years old.* A child between five and twelve should be in a separate time-out room. Since you will use time-out again and again, try a couple of different places and see which one is most effective.

Features of effective time-out places:

- Dull and boring for a child.

- No people; separated from other family members. (For safety, keep very young children within continual eye sight.)

- No toys, games, television,stereo, books, pets, and interesting objects.

- Safe, well-lighted, and not frightening.

- Can easily get there within 10 seconds.

Time-Out Places For

Two- to Four-Year-Olds

Jimmy And The Time-Out Chair

Three–year-old Jimmy was getting very impatient with his mother. He had been quietly playing with his toy cars for almost fifteen minutes! He wanted his mother's attention, but she was sitting at the kitchen table drinking coffee with a neighbor.

Carrying a big toy truck to his mother he said, *"You have to play with me."* His mother replied, *"Jimmy, when Mrs. Barton and I are finished talking, I will play with you."* *"No, play now!"* Jimmy commanded. He then raised the truck and brought it down on his mother's knee. *"Ouch! Time-out for hitting!"* she responded.

Immediately, she carried Jimmy to a large straight-back chair across the room. Then she set a portable timer for three minutes and placed it on the floor several feet from Jimmy's chair. Jimmy began to cry, scream, and carry on.

She explained to her startled neighbor, *"I've had a lot of trouble with Jimmy hitting me when he doesn't get his way. He used to hit me or try to hit me several times a day. Then I started using a time-out chair for hitting. This is the first time he's hit me in over two weeks. His behavior isn't perfect, but that time-out chair is really helping him to control his hitting."*

JIMMY

"Waah! I won't do it again! I want down! . . ."

A large straight-back chair is a good time-out place
for toddlers and preschoolers.

If your child is between two and four, an ideal place for
time-out is a large, straight-back chair. It's safer than using a
separate room for time-out. A large chair is dull and boring,
quickly available, and limits your child's activity and movement.
In addition, it's difficult for your child to quickly get down from a
large chair. An angry child can throw a small chair but is less able
to throw a large chair. Don't use a rocking chair, a small child's
chair, the sofa, an easy chair, a playpen, or your child's bed for
a time-out place.

You may place the time-out chair in the room with you, in
the adjoining room, or in the hall. For your child's safety, you
need to keep an eye on him, but only from the corner of your eye.
Don't actually make direct eye contact with your child. You want
him to feel that your are ignoring him during his brief time-out.
Don't let him catch you looking at him. One way to avoid giving
attention to your child is to pretend to read a magazine or
newspaper.

Quickly lift your toddler onto the time-out chair. Next,
place the ticking timer several feet from his time-out chair. After
the timer rings, lift your child down from the chair or tell him that
he may get down. Chapter 12 describes what to do if you think
that your child might try to "escape" from time-out.

Your child may sit or kneel on the chair, but not stand or jump, or touch her foot to the floor. Some children have tantrums on the chair. Consequently, it shouldn't be placed within kicking or hitting range of the wall or near dangerous or valuable objects. If you think that your child might fall off the large straight-back chair, place the chair on a soft rug.

Parents sometimes place the time-out chair in a corner of the room, turn it to the wall, and make their child face the wall. You may place the chair near a corner. However, don't demand that your toddler or preschooler face the wall or corner. It would take continuous effort on your part to make him face only one direction. Making him face the wall gives him a lot of your attention. Also, requiring that your child face the wall is overly harsh. Instead, let him face whichever direction he wants to face. However, do require that he either sit or kneel on the chair.

Your daughter shouldn't take any toys, dolls, or pets to time-out and shouldn't be able to see the television set from her chair. Tell her brother or sister not to pester or talk to her. Warn them that if they do, then they will be sent to a separate chair for time-out!

MISTAKES WHICH PARENTS MAKE WITH TIME-OUT

"Time-out isn't so bad after all! . . ."

How many time-out *mistakes can you find?*

Your child may call out from her chair, asking for attention and reassurance. She may say that you are a "bad Mama" or threaten to "run away from home." Actively ignore her and don't answer or make eye contact with her. Answering or looking at her are forms of attention and reduce the effectiveness of time-out. Resist feeling guilty or miserable while she is sitting on the chair. After all, time-out only lasts two to four minutes and will soon be over!

Some parents place their preschooler directly on the floor in the corner of a quiet room or in a semi-deserted hallway rather than using a time-out chair. A particular spot on the floor can be a good place for time-out if your child has learned to stay in one place. However, point to the exact spot where he is supposed to sit.

A TIME-OUT SPOT ON THE FLOOR

"That timer must be broken. I don't think it's ever going to ring. . . ."

A spot on the floor can be an effective time-out place for very young children.

Time-Out Places For Five- To Twelve-Year-Olds

Children who are between five and twelve should be placed in a separate room for time-out. It's safer to leave an older child alone in a time-out room than a preschooler who needs close monitoring.

Your home has several good time-out places such as a bathroom, laundry room, your bedroom, or a deserted utility room or hallway. Usually, the bathroom is the best place for time-out. This might sometimes cause an inconvenience to the rest of the family. Living with a problem child, however, can cause an even bigger inconvenience to family members! At first, your child might seem to enjoy playing in the water or making paper airplanes out of facial tissue. He may even say that he likes time-out in order to discourage you from using it. However, he will soon get tired of time-out. While waiting in time-out, a child frequently says that he needs to use the bathroom. Needing to use the bathroom isn't a problem if he is already there! The bathroom is an effective time-out place.

TIME-OUT IN HIS PARENTS' BEDROOM

*"Now why did Dad send me in here? Just because
I had a temper tantrum? . . ."*

Before you first begin using time-out, be sure to prepare the time-out room. Besides being dull and free of interesting objects, it should also be made safe. Any objects which might be dangerous, such as glass, sharp objects, medications or poisonous cleaning chemicals, should be removed from the room. After your child settles down and adjusts to time-out, you might return most of the objects to the room. Place the timer several feet outside the door so that your child can hear it while it is ticking and when it rings.

Don't Use Your Child's Bedroom

MISTAKES WHICH PARENTS MAKE WITH TIME-OUT

"She actually seems to enjoy time-out in her bedroom! . . ."

Your child's bedroom may seem to be the most "convenient" place for time-out. However, time-out won't work if you use your child's bedroom. A time-out place should be dull and boring with nothing interesting to do or see. Be effective when you use time-out. Resist the temptation to use your child's room as a time-out place.

Bradley's Bedroom For Time-Out

Bradley's parents complained that time-out wasn't effective in changing their son's behavior. When asked to describe how they used time-out, mom and dad revealed that Bradley's place for time-out was his bedroom complete with a radio, stereo, television, video games, computer, models, and toys. Many parents as well as children would enjoy spending time in such a time-out place!

After going to the time-out room, your child can do whatever he wants as long as he doesn't make a mess or destroy things. He can sit, stand, or walk around the room. If he makes a mess, by scattering objects around the room or spilling water on the floor, he must clean it up. If he damages something, he must help pay for it. Chapter 12 describes effective methods for easily handling such occasional behaviors rebellious to time-out.

Don't Use A Frightening Time-Out Place

MISTAKES WHICH PARENTS MAKE WITH TIME-OUT

"Time-out with Dageon the Dragon! . . ."

"Dageon The Dragon!"

Several years ago I counseled Mr. and Mrs. Meyers regarding ways they could help Bennie, their five-year-old son. Bennie was energetic and difficult to handle. He often grabbed toys away from his little sister or hit her.

We decided to use time-out for hitting and toy grabbing. Mr. and Mrs. Meyers were supposed to discuss this method between themselves but *not* use it until we had another appointment to discuss the correct steps. However, when we met the following week, I was shocked to learn that they had tried to frighten Bennie with time-out.

They told Bennie that if he hit his little sister or grabbed toys away from her, he would have to go to the basement for time-out. They further explained that a dragon named Dageon lived in their basement! Bennie became "hysterical," promised to be good, and pleaded with his parents not to send him to the basement.

Sensing Bennie's intense fear, Mr. and Mrs. Meyers stopped threatening to put Bennie in the basement. They also told him that there was no dragon there.

Time-out should never be scary. A frightening place for time-out is likely to cause emotional problems in a child. The purpose of time-out is not to frighten a child, but to *bore* him.

Main Points To Remember:

- A time-out place needs to be dull, boring, easily accessible, and safe.

- Use a large straight-back chair as a time-out place for children between two and four.

- Use a separate time-out room for children between five and twelve.

- Never use your child's bedroom as a time-out place. Time-out won't work if you do.

Chapter 8

Explaining Time-Out
To Your Child

"And when this timer rings you can come out. . . ."

Mom and Dad explaining time-out.

You and your spouse have selected a target behavior to be decreased and have chosen a boring place for time-out. Your next steps are to explain time-out and to wait for the target behavior to occur.

Introduce time-out when both you and your child are calm. Be sure that both you and your spouse join together in describing time-out. Your child needs to know that you *both* expect him to follow the rules about going to time-out and staying there until the timer rings.

Tell your child that both of you love him, but that his _____ behavior is causing problems for him and the family. He may quietly listen, or he may want to argue about time-out. Don't argue or debate whether you as parents have the right to put him in time-out.

Explaining Time-Out
To Two- To Four-Year-Olds

If your child is between two and four, it's best to demonstrate and practice time-out in addition to explaining it.

Helping Melissa To Stop Biting

Melissa is three years old. When she gets angry with other children, she threatens to bite and actually bites. Mom, dad, and Melissa are sitting at the kitchen table.

Mother: *"Melissa, your daddy and I both love you. We also want to help you. Remember yesterday when you got mad at James? You acted like you were going to bite him. Biting is against the rule."*

Melissa: *"Can I have a Coke?"*

Dad: *"Yes, in a couple of minutes. But right now we want to talk about biting and how to help you stop biting. If you bite or pretend to bite, you must sit on a chair. And you can't get down until this timer rings. When this timer rings, you may get off the chair."*

Melissa: *"Can I have a Coke now?"*

Mother: *"In a minute. Let me show you what happens when you bite. (Mother picks up Melissa and sits her on a large chair in the corner of the kitchen.) When Mommie puts you here, you have to stay here. You can sit or kneel on the chair, but you can't stand up. And you can't get down or you will be in big trouble! You have to sit here until the timer rings. (Father rings the timer.) Did you hear the timer ring? That means you may get down now. (Mother lifts Melissa from the chair and places her on the floor.) That is time-out."*

Melissa: *"Are you going to get me a Coke now?"*

Mother: *"Yes, I will get you a Coke. But you remember — when you bite or pretend to bite someone, mommie or daddy will sit you on a chair. You will have to stay there until the timer rings."*

Obviously, Melissa wasn't paying very close attention to her parents' explanation and demonstration of time-out. Melissa's parents will explain and demonstrate time-out two more times before actually using it. They could also demonstrate time-out by using one of Melissa's dolls or stuffed animals. Melissa will learn more about time-out by actually experiencing it after she bites or threatens to bite.

Explaining Time-Out
To Five- To Twelve-Year-Olds

If your child is older than four years of age, you will also need to explain time-out to him. Look at the following example of parents introducing time-out.

Telling Tim About Time-Out

Ten-year-old Tim has been hitting and threatening to hit other children and his younger brother when he gets angry with them. Other children are beginning to reject Tim because of his hitting and aggressiveness. Dad, Mom, and Tim are sitting around a small table.

Dad: *"Your mom and I want to talk with you about hitting your brother and other kids when you get mad. We both love you, and we want to help you with this problem. Hitting is causing problems for you, your brother, and the whole family."*

Tim: *"Bobby starts it most of the time! I just hit him back when he hits me or calls me names."*

Mother: *"Yes, sometimes Bobby hits you and calls you names. Even though he is only five years old, he still needs to behave himself. We are going to have a talk with him, too. But now let's talk about you and time-out."*

Dad: *"Every time you hit or threaten to hit someone, your mom or I will say time-out! That means that you must go to the bathroom immediately and stay there for 10 minutes. We will set this timer for 10 minutes. When you hear it ring, you may come out. You can't come out until it rings. If you don't go to time-out immediately or if you make a lot of noise in time-out, then you get extra minutes added on the timer. If you make a mess in time-out, then you get extra minutes on the timer and you have to clean up the mess before you come out."*

Tim: *"Who invented time-out anyway? What happens if I don't go to time-out? What happens if I leave time-out when I get ready?"*

Mother: *"Your dad and I expect you to go to time-out and stay there until the timer rings. If you don't go, then no television and no bicycle for the rest of the day, until you go to time-out. Then you have to stay in time-out for 10 minutes plus one extra minute for every minute you delay going. You might have to stay as long as 15 minutes if you don't go right away or if you leave time-out before the timer rings. When your dad and I tell you to go to time-out you must go! Your job is to go and stay there until the timer rings. Tim, do you have any questions about time-out?"*

Tim: *"Time-out is for little kids. It sounds silly. It sounds mean! Just spank me when I hit. And spank Bobby too. Will Bobby have to go to time-out?"*

Dad: *"If you hit each other, then you both have to go to time-out in separate places. Time-out will help you to stop hitting."*

Mother: *"We love you and Bobby. We expect both of you to mind us. And when we tell you to go to time-out, you must go immediately."*

When you tell your child about time-out, don't expect him to be enthusiastic about the plan. The next step for Tim's parents is to wait for the target behavior (hitting or threatening to hit) to occur.

When first beginning the time-out method, you might wonder if your child will cooperate by going to time-out and by staying there until the timer rings. An uncooperative response to time-out usually isn't difficult to handle. Chapter 12 describes what to do if you think your child might rebel against time-out.

Main Points To Remember:

- Describe time-out to your child.

- Tell your child that you love her and that you want to help her with a particular behavior problem.

- Don't be surprised if she acts annoyed or indifferent when you explain time-out.

- Demonstrate time-out several times if she is between two and four years old.

Chapter 9

Quickly Getting Your Child To Time-Out

"I don't want to go to time-out! I won't do it again! . . ."

Quickly *carry* your toddler to time-out.

This chapter will teach you the exact steps to follow in placing your child in time-out. It's important to get her there *quickly!* Swiftly placing her in time-out reduces her resistance to going to time-out. It also increases the effectiveness of this method of discipline. You want your child to see an immediate connection between her bad behavior and the distasteful experience of time-out.

By now, you have selected a boring place for time-out, explained time-out, and waited for the target behavior to occur. After your son or daughter displays the undesirable target behavior, follow the basic steps described in the box, "Four Steps For Using Time-Out."

Four Steps For Using Time-Out

After The

Target Behavior Occurs

1. Send or place your child in time-out and use no more than 10 words and 10 seconds.

2. Get the portable timer and set it to ring one minute for each year of your child's age. Place it within hearing distance of your child. (Chapter 10)

3. Wait for the timer to ring — don't give your child any attention while he waits. (Chapter 10)

4. Ask your child, after the timer rings, why he was sent to time-out. (Chapter 11)

Follow the basic steps with all children between two and twelve. You may need to practice and gain experience before automatically following the steps. Most parents have a natural tendency to scold their child before placing her in time-out. However, this is a mistake. Scolding, arguing, and talking to a child before placing her in time-out encourage her to argue, become emotionally upset, and delay getting to time-out.

Children try to avoid time-out by manipulating their parents. Children often protest, negotiate, blame other children, ask forgiveness, act indifferent, cry, plead, have a tantrum, or do something else to discourage you from sending them to time-out. Ignore all remarks and displays of emotion. Remain calm and immediately place her in time-out. If she wants to talk with you, she may do so after time-out. Be easy on yourself and your child; send her to time-out quickly. Use no more than 10 words and 10 seconds in doing so. You'll find that time-out gets easier and easier when you use it correctly!

Getting Two- To Four-Year-Olds To Time-Out

"For Spitting You Get Time-Out!"

Three-year-old Amanda was developing a bad habit of spitting or threatening to spit when angry with other children. Struggling with her sister over a toy, Amanda again introduced her effective weapon — spitting.

Mother immediately said, *"For spitting you get time-out!"* Quickly, Mother picked up Amanda from behind, walked across the room with her, and sat her on a large straight-back chair. Amanda said, *"I don't want to go to time-out! I won't do it again! . . ."* Ignoring her daughter's promise to stop spitting, Mother made no reply and simply left Amanda sitting on the time-out chair.

Good for Amanda's mother! She correctly followed the basic steps for placing her daughter in time-out. Carry two- and three-year-old children to the time-out chair. They are too young to quickly get there on their own. Some toddlers kick when carried to time-out, so be sure to carry them from behind. You can physically guide a four-year-old as she walks to a time-out chair. Never try to comfort or be affectionate with a child while you are taking her to time-out. Be stern or matter-of-fact and tell her, in 10 words or less, why she is being placed in time-out.

Getting Five- To Twelve-Year-Olds To Time-Out

Older children are *sent* to time-out and must travel there on their own. *Give an effective command when sending your child to time-out.* When the target behavior occurs, walk up to him, maintain a stern facial expression, and establish eye contact. Give a direct command to go to time-out and point in the direction of time-out. Study the illustration of "Mother Handling Back-Talk." Place the timer outside the door of the time-out room after your child arrives there.

MOTHER HANDLING BACK-TALK
1. BACK-TALK   2. TIME-OUT SIGN

"I don't have to make my bed or clean my room. Why do I have to do it? You aren't doing anything!"

"Time-out for back-talk"

3. POINTING TO TIME-OUT

"Go immediately to time-out!"

Use gestures to swiftly and effectively send the older child to time-out. Point in the direction of the time-out place while looking your child directly in the eye.

To signal the beginning of time-out, some parents use a "T" hand signal, the same time-out sign which is used in football.

Be sure to limit yourself to only 10 words and 10 seconds in sending your child to time-out.

Say only two things when placing the older child in time-out. *First*, label the misbehavior which your child demonstrated or state the rule he broke. Say, *"That was back-talk!"* or *"Hitting is against the rule!"* *Second*, command your child to go to time-out. Say, *"Go to time-out!"* or *"Go to time-out immediately!"* Say nothing else. Now might be a good time to review the section in Chapter 2 on "How To Give Effective Commands."

Most children between the ages of five and twelve learn to obey a clear command to go to time-out. If you think that your child might refuse to go, study Chapter 12 — "Common Time-Out Mistakes And Problems." Chapter 12 describes how you can handle any problems.

The basic steps for using the time-out method are always the same regardless of what your child did to deserve time-out. To become effective at using time-out, follow the basic rules described in this book and gain experience by actually using this method.

When beginning the time-out method, it will be helpful to occasionally review various chapters of this book. It would also be helpful to discuss your child's reactions to time-out with your spouse or with another person who is interested in your child.

Main Points To Remember:

- Place your child in time-out *quickly — using no more than 10 words and 10 seconds.*

- *Carry* toddlers and preschoolers to the time-out chair.

- *Send* the older child to the time-out place.

SOS Free Resources!
Over 20 practical resources
audio clips and video clips
for parents & counselors at
www.sosprograms.com

Chapter 10

The Timer And Waiting In Time-Out

"IMPATIENTLY" WAITING FOR THE TIMER TO RING

"Waaah! . . . I want down! . . . You're not my best friend! . . . Bad, mean Daddy! . . . I want my Mommie! . . . Doesn't anyone love me? . . . I don't like time-out . . . . Waaah!"

It's upsetting to see your child angry and emotional. What she says while in time-out may surprise or even shock you. Be sure that you and your spouse give each other lots of emotional support at these "difficult times." After time-out is over, give her all the attention she wants.

After placing your child in time-out, *set the timer one minute for each year of your child's age*. Next, place the timer within her hearing distance. She must wait until the timer rings before leaving time-out. Don't give her any attention while the timer is ticking.

One Minute For Each Year Of Age

Your child's age will determine how long she spends in time-out. In Chapter 6 you learned that children are to spend one minute in time-out for each year of age. If your child is two years old, set the timer for two minutes each time that you place her in time-out. If she is twelve years old, set the timer for twelve minutes. *Don't place your child in time-out for longer than one minute for each year of age!*

Some parents who mistakenly use both long and short periods of time-out find that the shorter periods of time-out become less effective. Do not use longer periods of time-out sometimes and shorter periods at other times. Parents often make the mistake of letting their anger toward their child's bad behavior determine how long their child will spend in time-out. Don't do this! Always use one minute for each year of age when placing your child in time-out. Only if your child rebels against time-out, should she spend more minutes in time-out than usual. Effectively handling your child's possible resistance to time-out is described in Chapter 12.

Where To Place The Timer

Place the timer out of reach, but within hearing distance of your child — about five to ten feet from the time-out place. The floor is a good spot for a timer. For children who attack timers following time-out, place the timer well out of their reach! Your child will learn to listen for the timer to signal when time-out is over. He will learn to depend on the timer rather than on your telling him when he may leave time-out. It's all right, but not necessary, that your child see the face of the timer. He should be able to hear it ticking and when it rings. Of course, never let your child handle or play with a timer while he is in time-out.

Toddlers and preschoolers, when they are *not* in time-out, often enjoy playing with a timer. Sometimes they put their dolls and animals on a time-out chair, next to a ticking timer. Allow them to practice their time-out skills because someday they too, will be parents!

Why A Portable Timer Is Necessary

Using a portable timer that can ring helps you to be consistent, organized, and fair when using the time-out method of discipline. Place the portable timer five to ten feet from your child after placing him in time-out. *Do not use the timer on your kitchen stove or microwave.* You will always need to bring the timer to the time-out place. Your child must actually be able to hear the timer ring. *The timer, not the parent, determines when the child gets out of time-out.* A portable timer is a must. It helps to remove the time-out power struggle between you and your child. *Always use a portable timer that can ring.*

DISCIPLINE *MISTAKES* PARENTS MAKE —
NOT USING A PORTABLE TIMER

"Mom, can I come out now? . . . Is the time up yet? . . ."

Your child will frequently call out to you if you don't use a portable timer. Failing to use a portable timer is a common mistake.

Reasons For Using A Portable Timer

- Timers can't be pestered and manipulated into ringing early.

- A timer doesn't forget to release your child from time-out. Parents sometimes do forget about a child in time-out.

- Your child learns to take responsibility for leaving time-out at the proper time.

- A ticking timer is a sign to other family members that a child is in time-out. Anyone giving attention to a child in time-out also runs the risk of being placed in time-out.

- Timers are "parent savers." When a timer is used, children stop asking parents when they may come out of time-out. Parents get more peace and quiet by using a portable timer.

What The Parent Does During Time-Out

Remember that your main objective after placing your child in time-out is to avoid giving her any attention. Most parents need to remain in the same room when their two- or three-year-old is in time-out. After placing your toddler or preschooler on the time-out chair, "command" her to stay there and say nothing else. Turn your head away from her and avoid eye contact. If a preschooler has a tantrum on the time-out chair, some parents pretend to look at a newspaper or magazine in order to avoid giving their child any attention. Your child will recognize that you are ignoring him when he is in time-out.

If your child is between five and twelve years old, she will be in a separate room for time-out, and you will have some time by yourself. Think about the steps you used in placing your child in time-out. Did you follow the basic rules and steps? If your spouse or another person who cares for your child is present, this might be a good time to discuss your child's behavior and your skill in using the time-out method. However, your child shouldn't hear such a discussion, because it might be annoying to her and encourage her to rebel against time-out.

WAITING IN TIME-OUT

"I AM MAD! Mom shouldn't have sent me here. I didn't hit my little sister that hard. I hate time-out. I could try to force Mom and Dad to let me out of here. . . . I could scream as loud as I can — they hate that. . . . I could kick the door. . . . I could run water all over the floor. . . . or maybe I'll wait my 10 minutes and then watch television."

The parents of ten-year-old Justin asked him why he often screamed and became so emotional while in time-out. He replied, *"It feels good to let it all out. . . . and I want you to feel as mad as I feel!"* Time-out was effective with Justin, but his parents sometimes had to give each other lots of emotional support during his time-outs!

When using time-out or any method of discipline, many parents begin to feel guilty, inadequate as parents, sorry for their child, or fear losing their child's love. Recognize that these feelings are natural for a parent and that all of us have doubts about our competence as parents. However, don't let these feelings prevent you from helping your child to improve his behavior. When you begin to seriously doubt yourself and feel significantly upset after disciplining your child, turn to Chapter 2 and read the section "Reasons Parents Don't Discipline Their Kids."

If your child rebels against the time-out method, then you need to study Chapter 12, "Common Time-Out Mistakes And Problems." This chapter will help you effectively handle your child's possible uncooperative response to the time-out method.

After the timer rings and time-out is over, what should you do or say to your child? Read on. The next chapter describes this final time-out step.

Main Points To Remember:

- *Set the timer one minute for each year of your child's age.*

- *Always use a portable timer that can ring.* Don't use the timer on your kitchen stove or microwave.

- Place the timer out of reach but within hearing distance of your child.

- Ignore your child until the timer rings.

Chapter 11

Talking With Your Child —
After Time-Out

AFTER TIME-OUT

*"I had to go to time-out because I hurt our puppy. .
. .Can I go outside and play now?"*

This chapter describes what you are to do and say after
time-out is over. The chapter also discusses the appropriate
time to decide if additional discipline besides time-out is needed.

A Talk With Thomas — After Time-Out

Mother was reading her book when the timer near
the bathroom rang. Seven-year-old Thomas had been in
time-out for mistreating his puppy. With timer in hand,
Thomas walks up to his mother. Let's listen to their brief
talk.

Mother: *"Hello, Thomas. Tell me, why did you have to go to time-out?"*

Thomas: *"I had to go to time-out because I hurt our puppy. . . . Can I go out and play now? I want to ride my bike down to Mike's house."*

Mother: *"Yes, hurting the puppy was why you went to time-out. If you want to go to Mike's house, that's fine. Be back in about an hour though."*

Thomas: *"Okay, see you in about an hour. Good-bye."*

Mother correctly handled this brief "after time-out" discussion.

The younger child, between two and eight years old, should say why he was sent to time-out. After he hears the timer ring and leaves time-out he should tell you what he did or the rule he broke that caused him to be sent to time-out.

Two and three year old children often forget why they were placed in time-out. If your child is two or three, use the following plan when the timer rings. Say to him, *"The timer rang, you may get down now"* Tell him, in a couple of words, the reason why he was placed in time-out. Ask him to repeat the reason. Then lift him from the chair and place him on the floor. Tell him he may go and play.

If your child is *four years old*, he will quickly learn to get off the chair by himself after hearing the timer ring. Help him to tell you why he was placed in time-out. If he tells you the correct reason, acknowledge what he says with something like, *"Yes, _____ was why you had to go to time-out."* That is all you should say. Normally, you shouldn't scold, make him say he is sorry, or have him promise to be good. He is free to go and usually neither of you will continue to be annoyed.

If the younger child doesn't remember why he was placed in time-out or gives you an incorrect reason, then you tell him why he was sent to time-out. After telling him the reason, say to him, *"Okay, I am going to ask you again. Tell me, why did you have to go to time-out?"* Continue this discussion until he can tell you why he was sent to time-out. When this "after time-out" discussion is over, your child is free to go.

Mark Puts Himself In Time-Out

A psychologist walked into her kitchen and was surprised to find Mark, her four year old son, sitting on the time-out chair. She was especially surprised since they were home alone and she had not placed him in time-out. He had put himself in time-out. She later asked him what he did to deserve time-out. He quietly replied, *"I don't want to talk about it."* Mother never did discover why Mark had put himself in time-out!

Don't insist that your child bring you the timer following time-out. This could lead to an unnecessary power struggle.

Don't insist that the older child, between nine and twelve, tell you why she had to go to time-out. The older child usually knows why you sent her to time-out. Making her tell about her misbehavior often leads to a power struggle. So "choose your battles" and don't insist that the older child, who is usually annoyed and resistive following time-out, describe her problem behavior.

If your child remains annoyed after leaving time-out, ignore her annoyance. She has a right to her feelings. If she wants to talk about whether or not she should have been sent to time-out, briefly listen to her. Avoid arguing, however.

Following time-out, parents sometimes learn that their child was actually "innocent" and didn't deserve to be put in time-out. When this happens to you, be sure to quickly apologize.

Some children act stubborn and delay leaving time-out after the timer rings. If this happens to you, read Chapter 12 - "Common Time-Out Mistakes And Problems." This section describes how to handle this minor problem.

Deciding Whether Additional Discipline Is Needed

Time-out immediately separates you and your child and gives both of you an opportunity to calm down. When used alone, time-out is normally enough correction for bad behavior. You can avoid yelling, scolding, making ineffective threats and getting upset. You have used one of the most effective methods for stopping bad behavior available.

You may think that time-out is not sufficient correction for a particular bad behavior. Perhaps another discipline method should also be used. You should consider an additional method of discipline only after you have an opportunity to calm down.

The time to make this decision is while your child is in time-out. Never announce an additional correction before placing your child in time-out.

You may decide to use scolding, natural consequences, logical consequences, or a behavior penalty in addition to time-out. These effective methods of mild discipline are discussed in Chapter 5. Usually, after your child is in time-out and you have a chance to cool off, you'll decide that time-out alone is sufficient. However, the correct time to decide if you need to use additional discipline is *while* your child is in time-out.

When your child has cooled off, and if he's willing to talk about his problem behavior, take advantage of this opportunity and talk to him. Help him to think of positive alternatives to his problem behavior. This discussion will be helpful in improving his future behavior.

Main Points To Remember:

- Children between two and eight years old should tell why they were sent to time-out.

- Avoid scolding your child following time-out.

- When time-out is used alone, it is usually sufficient discipline for bad behavior.

- The best time to decide if additional discipline is needed, is while your child is in time-out.

Chapter 12

Common Time-Out Mistakes And Problems

"Are you sorry for what you did? . . . Are you going to behave yourself when you come out? . . ."

Talking and arguing with a child *after* placing him in time-out is a common mistake which parents make.

The time-out method is easy to use, but it's also easy to make mistakes. *This chapter describes Nine Common Time-Out Mistakes which parents often make when using time-out.* These

---

The Video SOS Help For Parents helps educators and counselors to easily teach over 19 behavior management skills, including time-out. Educators and counselors are invited to order a free nine minute DVD sample from SOS Programs & Parents Press.

An eleven year old girl tells how she rebels against time-out and how her parents handle her rebellious behavior in the audio program, "How To Use Time-Out Effectively." Ordering information is at the end of this book.

mistakes reduce the effectiveness of time-out in changing your child's misbehavior. And making these nine mistakes also will cause your child to rebel against time-out.

   If your child tries to rebel against time-out by refusing to go or stay in time-out read the second part of this chapter, "If Your Child Rebels Against Time-Out." This section tells solutions to common time-out problems. *However, first be sure you aren't making any of the Nine Common Time-Out Mistakes.*

Nine Common Time-Out Mistakes Parents Make

Mistake #1   Talking or arguing with a child *after* placing him in time out.

Correct Way — *Ignore your child during time-out.*

Mistake #2   Talking or arguing with a child *before* placing him in time-out.

Correct Way — *Use no more than 10 words and 10 seconds in quickly getting your child to time-out.*

Mistake #3   Using a small child's chair, rocking chair, or couch as a time-out place for toddlers and preschoolers.

Correct Way — *Use a large straight-back chair as a time-out place for your toddler or preschooler.*

Mistake #4   Using a child's bedroom or an interesting place for time-out with older children.

Correct Way — *Use the bathroom or another boring place for time-out* with your older child.

Mistake #5   Keeping track of the time yourself or using a timer on the kitchen stove.

Correct Way — *Always use a portable timer that can ring — and place it out of reach, but within hearing of your child.*

TIME-OUT *MISTAKES* PARENTS MAKE

"Dad forgot to use a timer."

Mistake #6   Making a child apologize or promise to be good after he leaves time-out.

Correct Way — *After leaving time-out, your child can tell you the reason she was sent to time-out.* If she doesn't remember, you tell her what she did.

Mistake #7   Threatening to use time-out instead of using it.

Correct Way — *Actually use time-out each time the target behavior occurs.* Don't just threaten to use it.

Mistake #8   Trying to shame or frighten a child with time-out.

Correct Way — *Use time-out to bore your child and not to shame or frighten him.*

Mistake #9   Using very long, very short, or different periods of time for time-out.

Correct Way — *Time-out lasts one minute for each year of age.*

TIME-OUT *MISTAKES* PARENTS MAKE —
MERELY THREATENING TO USE TIME-OUT

"I've told you ten times to stay off the coffee table. If you get on the coffee table once more, you go to time-out! . . ."

Be sure to actually *use* time-out instead of *threatening* to use it. Merely threatening to use time-out is a common mistake.

If Your Child Rebels Against Time-Out

Be sure that you are not making any of the *Nine Common Time-Out Mistakes.* Read this following section if you are concerned about your child possibly rebelling against time-out. *If she resists time-out, select and follow a plan suited both to her age and to her particular type of rebellious behavior.*

Should your child resist time-out, you can manage this problem! Most children don't rebel beyond the first couple of weeks if their parents use time-out correctly. However, don't make any of the nine common time-out mistakes.

Your child may be clearly angry and upset when placed in time-out. Remember, she has several purposes for displaying anger and rebellious behavior. She wants to get your attention, to punish you for placing her in time-out, and to force you to stop using time-out. Resist your child's attempts to discourage you from being an effective parent!

"ESCAPING" FROM TIME-OUT

"I'm getting out of here!"

"Escaping" from time-out may be a problem when you first begin using the time-out method. However, this problem can be handled.

You have two major goals for using time-out. Your immediate goal is to abruptly stop your child's undesirable target behavior. Your long-term goal is to develop greater self-discipline and self-control in your child. Time-out is effective in helping to achieve both of these goals.

You love your child and naturally become upset when she is unhappy. Consequently, you and your spouse need to give help and emotional support to each other if your child becomes unhappy and hard-to-handle after being placed in time-out.

Parents should take specific steps to manage their child's resistance to time-out. If your child is *between two and four years old,* select a plan from the first half of this section to handle his rebellious behavior. If he is *between five and twelve years of age,* select a plan from the last part of this section.

Managing Two- To Four-Year-Olds
Who Rebel Against Time-Out

Rebellion #1 Delaying or refusing to go to time-out.

Your Plan — Quickly carry all toddlers and preschoolers to the time-out chair, even those who don't resist going to time-out. Most four-year-olds will eventually learn to walk to time-out on their own.

Rebellion #2 Making noise in time-out. Your child may call out to you, cry, or have a tantrum on the time-out chair.

Plan A — Ignore your child. Turn away and avoid eye contact while he is in time-out. Noisemaking in time-out will usually decrease by itself if you consistently ignore it.

Plan B — If your child is three or four years old, tell him that if he continues making noise, you'll add minutes on the timer. If he is noisy when the timer rings, set the timer for one or two extra minutes.

Comments — Noisemaking is usually the only type of rebellious behavior that may continue for several weeks or longer. Recognize that your child is trying to force you to stop using time-out by making noise in time-out.

Rebellion #3 "Escaping" from the time-out chair. Your child steps down from the large straight-back chair and runs off.

Plan A — Repeatedly (ten times if necessary) retrieve your child and place him back on the chair. Stand next to the chair and harshly command him to stay on the chair. Say, *"Don't you dare get off that chair!"* If he continues trying to escape, consider the following alternative plans.

Plan B — Place your hand firmly on his leg or shoulder and look away from him. Command him to stay on the chair. Say nothing else.

Plan C — Kneel behind the time-out chair and firmly hold your child on the chair. Cross his arms on his chest and grasp his wrists. Be sure that you are using a large time-out chair. Tell him that he will be released when he stops trying to get away. Say nothing else. Before beginning this method, you must be determined to win this power struggle.

Plan D — Firmly hold your child in your lap and sit in the chair yourself. Tell your child that you will start the timer after he stops trying to get away. You must be determined to win before beginning this method.

Comments — If the above plans are not effective, you will need to consult a family counselor regarding ways to help your child to improve his behavior. Refer to Chapter 22, "When And How To Get Professional Help."

Most children will stay on a time-out chair when commanded to do so. When escaping from time-out is a problem, most parents find that this problem rarely lasts more than one or two weeks after beginning the time-out method. Always use a large straight-back chair and a portable timer.

Rebellion #4 **Not leaving time-out after the timer rings.**

Your Plan — Tell your child that the timer rang and that it's okay to get off the chair. Then use *active ignoring* or leave the room.

Rebellion #5 **After leaving the time-out chair, your child continues to cry or scream.**

Your Plan — If your *two- or three-year-old child* continues to scream or cry loudly after leaving time-out, walk out of the room and don't give her any attention. If your *four-year-old child* continues to cry loudly or verbally abuse you after leaving time-out, place her back in time-out for another four minutes. Do this only once.

Rebellion #6 **After leaving time-out, your child is annoyed with you, but does not cry or scream.**

Your Plan — Ignore your child's annoyance. Don't insist that he be pleasant after leaving time-out. He has a right to his own feelings.

Rebellion #7 **Child intentionally hurts herself while on the time-out chair.**

Comments — A child who intentionally hurts herself usually has demonstrated this same behavior at other times when angry or disciplined. A child who hurts herself when corrected has "accidentally" learned this undesirable behavior. This behavior can be changed, but you may need to work with a family counselor. A counselor can give you specific suggestions suited to your child.

Managing Five- To Twelve-Year-Olds
Who Rebel Against Time-Out

Rebellion #1 **Delaying or refusing to go to time-out.** Your child does not immediately go to time-out or refuses to go.

Your Plan — If you child delays or resists going to time-out, tell him that he must go immediately or he will have to spend additional minutes in time-out. For each ten seconds he delays going to time-out, add one more minute on the timer. *Silently* count from one to ten in order to keep track of ten seconds. Then add as many as five additional minutes on the timer.

After you add five additional minutes on the timer, warn your child that he will receive a particular *behavior penalty* (a loss of certain privileges) if he does not immediately go to time-out. After giving this warning, silently count from one to ten. If he does not go to time-out by the time you reach ten, announce the behavior penalty and walk off. Do not count out loud, become angry, or argue. Simply walk off. See Chapter 5 for a description and examples of behavior penalty.

Consider the following example of how a mother dealt with her ten-year-old daughter, Kelly. Kelly was attempting to avoid going to time-out by arguing with her mother.

Mother refused to argue and said, *"Kelly, you already have ten minutes of time-out. Now you have one more minute for not going right away. That's a total of eleven minutes."* (Mother pauses and counts silently to ten.) "Okay, you now have eleven minutes plus one more minute and that makes twelve minutes." Kelly stopped arguing, turned, and reluctantly walked off to time-out.

If Kelly had continued to delay going to time-out, her mother would have added as many as five additional minutes to the original ten minutes. If Kelly had not gone to time-out by then, her mother would have announced that Kelly's privilege of watching television for the rest of the day was revoked — a *behavior penalty*. After announcing this particular penalty to

Kelly, her mother would have walked off and refused to discuss the matter any longer. If Kelly had wanted to watch television that day, she first would have had to go to time-out for fifteen minutes.

Comments — If your child refuses to go to time-out, give her a *behavior penalty*. However, also permit her to go to time-out later in the day in order to remove the behavior penalty. For children five to twelve, a behavior penalty backs up time-out.

When you first use time-out with your child, you and your spouse should be present so that your child knows that you agree with each other. If she delays going to time-out, you might need additional practice in giving *effective commands* — a skill discussed in Chapter 2. Don't scold or argue with your child if she resists going to time-out. Children who resist going to time-out usually resist only the first week or two.

MAKING NOISE IN TIME-OUT

"I don't like time-out!"

Some children attempt to rebel against time-out by making noise or having a tantrum. Be calm! You can handle this problem also.

Rebellion #2 **Making noise in time-out.** Your child may continuously call out to you, cry loudly, stomp his feet, say he hates everyone, or have a full tantrum.

Plan A — Ignore your child, stay away from the time-out room, and do not try to calm him down. Don't scold, reassure, or answer your child. Be sure not to reward his noisemaking by paying attention to this behavior. The best way to decrease noisemaking is to use *active ignoring* — to withdraw all attention from your child.

Plan B — Add extra minutes on the timer for noisemaking. If your child is noisy when the timer rings, reset the timer for two more minutes.

Comments — Remember that your child's purpose for making noise is to get your attention, make you angry, and force you to stop using time-out. Don't get angry or scold him for making noise, as this rewards this undesirable behavior. Simply ignore him and set extra minutes on the timer. Be sure that you're using a *portable timer* so that your child doesn't learn to keep calling out to you to "see if he can come out now."

Making noise in time-out is one type of rebellious behavior that may continue for some time. Many parents go to a distant part of their house or apartment to avoid the noise. Going to another part of the house until the noise stops is a good idea since this reduces stress on you and also ensures that your child will receive no attention.

Time-Out At The Motel

Although in a motel, mother and father needed to handle their six-year-old son's temper tantrum. They placed him in time-out in their motel bathroom. However, his crying was so loud and obnoxious that they had to leave their motel room.

They found themselves standing on the sidewalk outdoors until their son's time-out was over! Mother and father correctly handled their son's noisemaking by actively ignoring it.

Rebellion #3 **"Escaping" from the time-out room.** Your child leaves time-out before the timer rings.

Your Plan — For each ten seconds that your child is absent from the time-out room, one more minute is added to the timer, up to a maximum of five additional minutes. If she doesn't return to time-out, or is absent more than one or two minutes, she receives a *behavior penalty* (such as no television for the rest of the day). Refuse to get angry, announce the behavior penalty, and walk off. Don't argue with your child. Be sure to follow through with the behavior penalty that you announce.

Comments — Escaping from time-out is usually not a problem. If it is a problem, it rarely lasts past the first two weeks.

Rebellion #4 **Making a mess in the time-out room.** Your child may scatter objects about the room or spill water on the floor.

Your Plan — Be matter-of-fact and require your child to clean up the mess before he may leave the room. Don't act shocked or scold.

Comments — Recognize that making a mess in time-out is just another attempt at punishing you or forcing you to stop using time-out. The day after placing his nine-year-old son in the bathroom for time-out, one father discovered that his new aerosol container of shaving cream was empty! His son apparently had emptied the entire container into the bathroom sink and rinsed the lather down the drain!

Rebellion #5 **Damaging the time-out room.**

Plan A — Your child must clean up the room and help pay for damages. One way that he may pay for damages is to do extra chores at home. You may need to select and arrange another room for time-out, a room that is safe but less easily damaged. However, do not use your child's bedroom.

Plan B — You may need to meet with a family counselor for professional help to determine specific methods to help a child who loses control when disciplined. Refer to Chapter 22, "When And How To Get Professional Help."

Rebellion #6 **Not leaving time-out after the timer rings or your child says he "likes" time-out.**

Your Plan — If your child doesn't leave time-out after the timer rings say, *"The timer rang. You can come out now if you want to, or you can stay in there — whatever you want to do."* Then turn and walk away. Say nothing else. A bright child may say that she "likes" time-out. Don't take her statement seriously. This is just another attempt at manipulating her parent into not using time-out.

Rebellion #7 **After leaving time-out, your child continues to scream, yell, and cry.**

Your Plan — Immediately place your child back into time-out for another full period of time-out.

Rebellion #8 **After leaving time-out, your child is annoyed with you, but does not cry or scream.**

Your Plan — Don't insist that your child be cheerful after leaving time-out. Ignore his annoyance. Be sure that you don't appear or act angry after time-out is over. Also, don't "apologize" for timing-out your son or daughter.

Rebellion #9 **Your child intentionally hurts herself while in time-out.**

Comments — A child who intentionally hurts herself usually has engaged in this behavior at other times when angry or disciplined. She is trying to punish and control her parents. It's especially important to help your child to overcome this pattern of self-destructive behavior. You probably will need to work with a family counselor who can tailor recommendations and a plan to fit your child. Read Chapter 22, "When And How To Get Professional Help."

You will need professional assistance if your child physically attacks you or runs out of the house to avoid time-out. If your child refuses to go to time-out and ignores the consequent *behavior penalty*, day after day, you may need to get professional help.

Main Points To Remember:

- Used correctly, the time-out method is effective and easy to use.

- Used *incorrectly*, the time-out method is ineffective and difficult to use.

- Be sure that you are not making any of the *Nine Common Time-Out Mistakes*. Time-out won't work if you are making these mistakes.

- If your child rebels against time-out, select a plan from this chapter to effectively handle her resistance. Be sure to use a plan suited to her age.

Section Three

FURTHER APPLICATIONS OF YOUR PARENTING SKILLS

This section of SOS examines more methods for helping your child. We'll study skills for managing bad behavior away from home, and how to use *points, tokens,* and *parent-child contracts* to improve a variety of behaviors.

Steps for *timing-out two children* and for *timing-out toys* are described. You can use these two variations of the time-out method as additional ways to reduce your child's behavior problems.

You'll learn skills for handling your child's aggressive and dangerous behavior. You'll also learn how to use *reflective listening* to help your children better understand, express, and control their feelings, emotions, and behavior.

The final chapter in this section, looks at solutions to more childhood problems such as hyperactivity and resisting chores. This chapter also teaches more parenting skills such as *"racing the timer"* and using a *"resting chair."*

Let's look at these additional ways for helping your child!

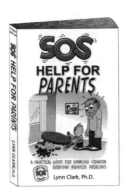

Chapter 13

Managing Bad Behavior Away From Home

"Put it back! . . ."

"NO! I WANT IT!"

A child's obnoxious, demanding behavior in public
places is embarrassing and difficult to handle.

When you and your child are away from home, does his
bad behavior ever embarrass you? Are you able to handle his
loud complaining or persistent demands while visiting friends or
shopping together? Do you ever think to yourself, *"I'll never take
him anywhere again!"*

There is hope for you and your child! You can improve your
child's embarrassing behavior away from home. Use the methods
described in this chapter and be more effective and confident
when you and your child visit friends and relatives, shop, and go
other places together.

To be an effective parent, you need to be a "well armed parent" — equipped with a variety of sound discipline skills. Parents whose only discipline skill is "nagging and scolding" will do a lot of that on trips away from home with their child!

Begin with the parenting skills that you have already learned. Especially important skills and methods for managing behavior away from home include — frequently praising and commenting on good behavior and failing to reward bad behavior. Consider occasionally using logical consequences and behavior penalty, and sometimes employing time-out or variations of time-out. Glance back over the previous chapters to review some of these parenting skills.

A POCKET-SIZE TIMER

A pocket-size timer is convenient when visiting friends or traveling.

Visiting The Homes Of Friends And Relatives

Prepare your child for visits away from home. Ask her to take along several small toys or books to read. Be sure that she has something interesting to do while you're talking with adults. *Before leaving home, explain to your child the behavior you expect.* Tell her the exact misbehavior (such as back-talk or angry screaming and screeching) which will result in time-out or in a particular behavior penalty (for example, no television later). If she behaves well, praise that behavior immediately or while you are returning home.

Use immediate time-out or "delayed time-out" to help manage misbehavior when you and your child are visiting. *Before you use time-out away from home, you should be comfortable and consistent when using it in your own home and when guests are present.* In addition, your child should be cooperating with the time-out method, rather than rebelling against it.

When away from home, give your children one warning before sending them to time-out or telling them that they have "chalked up" a time-out. Just like you do at home, use one minute of time-out for each year of your child's age. Get a pocket-size timer for trips away from home.

After you arrive at the home of relatives or friends notice any dull, boring places that you might use for time-out! Almost any place that is free of people and interesting activities will do.

PROBLEMS PARENTS FACE — OTHERS
INTERFERE WITH DISCIPLINE

"SAVE ME, GRANDMA! Momma is going to put me in time-out! . . ."

Some relatives or friends may interfere when you attempt to discipline your child in their presence. Ask you spouse for emotional support and help in coping with these well-meaning relatives or friends.

Some parents successfully use the backseat of their car as a time-out place when they are away from home, especially if their child is usually noisy while in time-out. Place your child in the backseat, and you sit in the front seat or stand outside the car. If you stand outside be sure that you keep the car keys. Ignore her and make sure that she doesn't have any toys while in time-out.

If possible, use an immediate time-out rather than a delayed time-out. Immediate time-outs are more effective in reducing bad behavior. If you can't send your child to time-out right away, then use delayed time-out. *A child should go directly to delayed time-out after returning home.* Be sure that she goes to time-out immediately. *Delayed time-out should only be used with children who are four and older.*

Katie Almost Chalks Up A *Delayed Time-Out*

Seven-year-old Katie and her parents are visiting friends. It's after 10:00 p.m. and father tells Katie again that it's time to go home. Katie announces that she is not ready to leave yet, and she backs up her announcement with whining, tears, and angry crying!

Father: *"Katie, ten minutes ago I told you it's time to go home. Go put your shoes and coat on now!"*

Katie: *"No, I don't want to go! I want to play some more! You never let me play when I want to! You always make me go home!" (Whining turns into loud crying).*

Father: *"I am going to give you one warning. Stop crying and get your shoes and coat on right now — or it's time-out when you get home!"*

Katie: *"All right! You don't have to be so mean." (Katie stops crying and puts on her shoes and coat). "Can we come back next week? I want to play some more."*

Father: *"We had a good time tonight. Yes, maybe all of us can get together next week."*

Father was effective in handling Katie's tantrum and refusal to return home. He warned her once and told her that if she didn't mind him, he would give her a delayed time-out.

Stores, Shopping Malls, And Restaurants

When getting ready for a shopping trip, be specific when telling your child how you want her to behave. When shopping, consider her age. Be reasonable about the length of time that you expect her to "tag along" without becoming tired, whining, and misbehaving.

If your child isn't tired, but simply acts like a pest while you are in a grocery store, shopping mall, or family restaurant, consider using a variation of time-out. In grocery stores, a good time-out place is usually in a corner or a side aisle. Point to a safe spot on the floor for your child to sit. Turn your back, pretend "to look at groceries," and don't give her any attention. If she is very young, stand near her. If she is older, stand further away. But for safety's sake, always keep your child in sight.

At shopping malls, benches make excellent time-out places. Have your child sit on a bench. If your child is older, pick another bench for yourself. You'll both get a break from each other and an opportunity to rest! For time-out in restaurants, such as McDonald's, an older child can briefly sit alone at a separate table.

Most children who are in a public place will sit quietly while in time-out. However, if your child is crying loudly, select a time-out place outside the store, such as the backseat of your car. You may also choose delayed time-out as an alternative.

*"Be Quiet Or You Can't Play
With Your Superman Suit!"*

Twice each week my five-year-old son, Eric, accompanied my wife to the doctor's office where she got her allergy shots. Eric spent his time making noise and running in the waiting area. My wife spent her time trying to quiet him.

Finally my wife said, *"Eric, you are very noisy when we are at the doctor's office. Most of the people there are sick and waiting to see the doctor. In the future, each time that you're running and noisy, you won't be allowed to play with your Superman suit for the rest of the day."* Eric lost the privilege of playing with his Superman suit only one time. His favorite activity was playing with his Superman suit. After receiving this penalty, he immediately settled down. My wife rarely had difficulty with unruly behavior during their future visits to the doctor's office.

My wife was effective in reducing our son's bad

behavior while they were away from home. She used the method of *behavior penalty* — in this case, withdrawing a favorite activity or privilege.

When your child behaves badly in public, be sure that you don't accidentally reward and, consequently, strengthen that bad behavior. An example of rewarding bad behavior is allowing your daughter to keep the candy bar she grabbed while standing in the checkout line. Quickly returning home because your child wants to go home and has a temper tantrum is another instance of rewarding bad behavior. However, remember that young children tire easily. Don't make the shopping trip too long.

Reward your child if she behaves while you are shopping. Give her praise or let her get a piece of gum from the gum machine as you leave the grocery store, but only if she has been good. Before leaving the department store, let her look at something that she wants to see, such as the animals in the pet department or dolls in the toy department.

In The Car

A miserable experience for parents is to ride in a car with a backseat of noisy, fighting children. Help prevent bad behavior by carefully organizing the car as well as the trip. Be sure that everyone (you, too!) wears a seat belt. Wearing seat belts reduces behavior problems. Seat belts prevent children from crowding too closely together and invading each other's space. The trip is not only more pleasant, but safer for everyone. On long trips, one parent might sit in the backseat to keep the children from "roughhousing" or annoying each other. Ask your children to select toys, books, or a game to take in the car.

Before leaving on a car trip, you can often anticipate the likelihood of misbehavior occurring. If you suspect problems, tell your children in advance that a particular consequence will occur if they misbehave in the car. Also tell them that they will get only one warning before receiving a consequence. An appropriate consequence could be a *delayed time-out* or a mild *logical consequence* such as stopping the car for several minutes until the misbehavior ends. Pulling the car off the road for five or ten minutes is more effective if you are traveling somewhere appealing to children — such as the beach or a park.

When a child gets a *delayed time-out*, she must go to time-out as soon as possible, usually as soon as you return home.

However, on a long car trip, she should do her delayed time-out as soon as you stop at a rest area along the highway. She briefly stays in the car for her time-out after the rest of the family leave the car. However, you should stay near the car.

Outdoor Play Activities

At the park, zoo, swimming pool, and on camping trips, it's easy to use *immediate time-out* to manage your child's misbehavior. Point to a safe place for your child to sit — on a park bench, on a large rock, by a tree, at the corner of the playground, or in the backseat of your car. Immediate time-out is easy to use and it's effective when parents follow through with it.

One mother was amazed because *immediate time-out* worked so well in controlling the "brat behavior" of her nine-year-old son while they were at the swimming pool. After receiving two immediate time-outs, he stopped splashing and dunking younger children. His behavior toward other children improved and his mother's relationship with other mothers greatly improved. Previously, she had tried scolding and yelling, but these methods were completely ineffective. In fact, he made faces at her when she scolded him. She considered taking him home if he misbehaved (a logical consequence), but this would punish her too! Time-out was a mild consequence, but it was completely effective in eliminating her son's brat behavior at the pool.

If your child misbehaves near your house or apartment, it isn't necessary to have him come indoors for time-out. Have him sit some specific place such as the front steps. Then find the timer and place it within hearing distance.

Main Points To Remember:

- Be sure to frequently reward your child's good behavior with attention and praise. Do this at home and away from home.

- Before leaving home, explain to your child the behavior you expect.

- In the home of friends, use time-out as you do in your own home.

- In public places, consider using *immediate time-out, delayed time-out,* or *behavior penalty*.

SOS Free Resources!
Over 20 practical resources
audio clips and video clips
for parents & counselors at
www.sosprograms.com

Chapter 14

Using Points, Tokens, And Contracts

"Let's see. You get one point for straightening your room and one point for clearing the table after supper. I'm really proud that you earned these points! . . ."

Children enjoy working for points. When Susan gets enough points, she will exchange them for a small doll.

A Point-Reward Program Helps Susan

Seven-year-old Susan had several problem behaviors which bothered her parents. She often left clothes, toys, and books scattered about her room. Mr. and Mrs. Madison tried letting her "live in the clutter" (a natural consequence) but that didn't bother Susan a bit. She seemed to enjoy the mess.

When asked to help with simple chores, Susan often complained, said that she was *"too tired,"* or whined that *"Chores aren't any fun."* Her parents tried nagging and scolding. However, Susan continued resisting their requests.

Although frustrated, Susan's parents began a special reward incentive program and within two weeks Susan's behavior greatly improved. How did Mr. and Mrs. Madison help their daughter change? They used a point-reward program. Read on to see how to develop such a program.

Material rewards (a small toy) and *activity rewards* (going to the park) help motivate children to improve their behavior. Provide a way for your child to earn tokens, points, or check marks to purchase rewards. After earning a number of points or tokens, your child can exchange them for a particular reward that she wants.

Earning *tokens* motivates adults as well as children. If you have a job outside your home, you earn tokens (in the form of paychecks and money), which you exchange for material rewards (a pizza, new shoes) and activity rewards (going to the movies or on vacation). To help your child develop a new behavior or habit, you sometimes need to offer her more than praise and attention. Once her new behavior is well established, you can phase out and eventually discontinue this special incentive program.

Parents can use *token rewards* with children who are four or five years old. *Point-rewards* are effective with children six to twelve. *Parent-child contracts,* another type of special incentive plan, are used with children from seven or eight through adolescence. Let's look closer at these special programs.

Offering Point-Rewards

Follow six steps in putting together an effective point-reward program for your child:

1. Select a target behavior.
2. Make a *point-reward calendar.*
3. Write a *menu of rewards.*
4. Keep track of the points earned and spent.
5. Adjust the reward program.
6. Discontinue the program.

1. Select one or more target behaviors that you want improved. You must be able to pinpoint and actually count the behavior that you want increased such as clearing the table after meals.

Describe the target behavior in positive rather than negative terms. For example, Mr. and Mrs. Madison asked Susan to "have a clean bedroom" rather than to "stop having a messy bedroom." They also listed several other behaviors such as emptying the trash, regularly brushing her teeth, etc.

Susan's Point-Reward Calendar

For Improving *Several* Behaviors

POINTS EARNED							
List of Good Behavior (and possible points)	**S**	**M**	**T**	**W**	**T**	**F**	**S**
Clean bedroom, check 6:00 p.m. (2 points)	0	II	II				
Clear dinner table (each meal, 1 point)	I	II	II				
Empty trash by 6:00 p.m. (1 point)	I	0	I				
Brush teeth (each meal, 1 point)	II	I	III				
Be home on time after school (2 points)	0	0	II				
Tantrum-free day (2 points)	0	0	II				
TOTAL POINTS EARNED	IIII	IIII I	IIII IIII IIII				

This calendar provides a record of several kinds of behaviors for one week. Post a new calendar each week.

At the end of each day, total the number of points your child has earned. Draw marks through the points on the bottom line when your child spends those points.

2. Make a *point-reward calendar*. Write down the target behaviors on this calendar. Also, write down the time when you will check to see if the behavior has occurred or not. Next to each target behavior, list one or more points that your child might earn for that behavior. After you prepare the calendar, post it in a conspicuous place if your child is young. Older children usually want the calendar put in a nonpublic place.

Examine the point-reward calendar which Mr. and Mrs. Madison and Susan made. They designed a calendar for recording several behaviors at one time. However, it's usually easier for parents to learn how to use a point-reward program by first focusing on only one problem behavior. Study the "Point-Reward Calendar For Improving *One* Behavior."

Point-Reward Calendar

For Improving *One* Behavior

POINTS EARNED						
Good Behavior (and possible points): *Room is neat. This means bed is made and all clothes, toys, and books are put in their proper places. Check at 7:30 a.m. (1 point). Check at 6:00 p.m. (1 point).*						
S	**M**	**T**	**W**	**T**	**F**	**S**
First Week	*0*	*I*	*0*	*II*	*I*	*II*	*II*
Second Week	*II*	*II*					
Third Week							

This calendar records *one* behavior for *several* weeks. At the end of the third week, post a new calendar.

When your child spends a point, draw a red mark or slash through that point. Points without slash marks are points not yet spent. Encourage your child to spend her points rather than save them because it is more reinforcing for your child.

3. Write down a *menu of rewards* and post it near the point-reward calendar. A *menu of rewards* is a list of small *material rewards* and *activity rewards* (privileges) which your child desires. Ask her what she would like to work for. Susan said that she wanted to work for a comic book, a particular doll, a trip to McDonald's, and so on.

Sample Menu Of Rewards

Menu of Rewards	
Reward	Cost in points
Comic book	4
Trip to McDonald's	12
Dad plays ping-pong with me	4
Soft drink from refrigerator	6
Package of sugarless gum	3
Make popcorn	9
Staying up till 9:30 p.m. on school night	7
Trip to park	8
Ice cream bar from freezer	6
Play video game with parent	4
Trip to get pizza	15
Small toy (less that $7.00)	30

This menu lists various material rewards and activity rewards. It also lists how many points or tokens your child must pay for each reward. Post this menu next to the point-reward calendar.

After you and your child list possible rewards, then you decide how many points each reward will cost. You don't want the rewards to be too easy or too hard to earn because your daughter might lose enthusiasm for the program. After you gain experience using a menu of rewards, it will be easier to determine the appropriate cost for new rewards. It's best to begin a point-reward program using small rewards that don't cost your child very much and don't cost you very much! She needs the opportunity to frequently earn rewards.

4. Keep track of the points as your child earns and spends them. When your child earns a point, record it on the calendar with enthusiasm. Give lots of praise for her good behavior and the points she earns.

Encourage her to spend her points rather than save them so that she will enjoy the program more. After she spends a point and receives a reward, place a slash mark through that point.

When your child has earned enough points to select a reward, let her purchase the reward as soon as possible. If she is as young as six or seven, be particularly quick to help her exchange points for a reward.

5. Make adjustments within the program so that it works better. Keep the old calendars after posting new ones. By looking at these old calendars, both of you can see how much progress she has made in improving her behavior.

The calendars tell you how well your program is working. To improve the program, make clearer definitions of what she must do to earn points and add new rewards to the menu. Be sure that you give her these new rewards only if she earns them. If she gets rewards without working for them, why should she work?

Some parents use *fines* for bad behavior — they take away points that their child has earned. However, your child might get discouraged with the program if she loses points after earning them. Combine other methods of discipline for bad behavior, such as logical consequences or time-out, with the point-reward program for good behavior. For example, Susan's parents placed her in time-out when she had a tantrum. When she had a tantrum-free day, she earned two points. Her tantrums rapidly decreased.

6. Phase out the program. Don't keep a point-reward program indefinitely, just until your child's behavior improves. Tell your child that the point-rewards helped her to make improvements in her behavior and that you are proud of these improvements. Continue to praise her improved behavior and discontinue the point-reward program. Parents can phase out the program in several ways. Omit giving points when she fails to ask for them. Increase the amount of time between earning the points and exchanging them for rewards. Consider having a party for her since she has "graduated" from the program. Take her and the family to a special place to eat that she has chosen.

GIVING TOKEN REWARDS

A clear plastic container is a good place for young children to keep their tokens.

Most four- and five-year-olds prefer to earn tokens rather than points because they can touch and hold tokens and carry them around. Use poker chips, play money, or other small objects as tokens. Don't let your child handle or play with any tokens unless she has earned them. She will need a container, perhaps a plastic jar or cup, for her tokens. If she is four or five years old, encourage her to keep the token container in a special place so she won't lose her tokens.

You need to select a target behavior and make up a menu of rewards. Give your child tokens rather than points for her good behavior. For preschoolers, draw or cut out pictures of rewards (a toy, an ice cream bar) for the menu of rewards. Next to the picture of each reward, draw another picture showing the number of tokens she must pay for that reward.

When the desirable target behavior occurs, give your child a token. When she has earned enough tokens, she can purchase a reward. A token-reward program is simple to operate once it's set up and after your child learns that she can exchange tokens for "goodies."

Tokens And Ice Cream Bars

Four-year-old Ann rarely answered or came when her mother called her. Mother decided to use a token-reward program and to give Ann a token each time that she came when called. Ann said that she wanted to work for ice cream bars from the freezer. Mother said that each ice cream bar would cost five tokens.

Ann earned one or two ice cream bars a day for a week. Mother then slowly discontinued the token-reward program. However, Ann continued to come when called.

Writing Parent-Child Contracts

A parent-child contract is a written agreement between you and your child. All parties join together in identifying a problem, discussing and negotiating a solution, clarifying responsibilities, signing the agreement, and following through with the agreement.

Contracts are used with children as young as seven or eight. These problem-solving tools are especially useful to families with adolescents.

Think of a problem that your family is experiencing. Consider negotiating a parent-child contract to resolve it.

"He's Lonely By Himself"

"He's lonely out there all by himself," eight-year-old Paul pleaded. *"He gets cold in the garage. See, he always tries to make a nest to keep warm. I want him in my room."*

Mrs. Carr has been listening to these same insistent, monotonous statements from Paul for the past two weeks. She was tired of hearing Paul say that he wanted his gerbil in his room. She felt sorry because Paul and his gerbil were separated. However, she knew that she would also get tired of cleaning up after the gerbil if Paul moved it inside the house.

Paul's father suggested that the three of them write up an agreement spelling out Paul's responsibilities for keeping the gerbil's cage clean. Mr. Carr said that the contract should also state the consequences if Paul didn't keep his part of the bargain. If Paul didn't regularly clean the cage, then the gerbil would be returned to the garage.

A contract was written, dated, and signed by all three family members. The Carr family discovered a new way for handling family disagreements — parent-child contracts.

PARENT-CHILD CONTRACTS —
SOMETIMES AN EFFECTIVE SOLUTION

*"I'll do it. I'll clean his cage every week. And you
and Mom will let me keep him in my room. Let's all
sign the contract now! . . ."*

Follow four steps in writing and using a contract:

1. Identify a problem.

2. Negotiate a solution with your child.

3. Write down the agreement.

4. Sign the contract and follow it.

1. Identify a problem. Contracts usually focus on resolving *a single, clear problem* concerning a family, such as Paul keeping a gerbil in his room. Be sure your contract doesn't specify vague, hard to measure objectives such as, "an improved attitude." Contracts are successfully used to encourage children to come home promptly after school and to set a time for doing homework each day. Negotiate a contract with your child before he gets a new pet. It's important to negotiate a contract before he receives a potentially hazardous object such as a BB gun, archery equipment, or a chemistry set. The contract should state that he will temporarily lose the object if he becomes careless with it.

Completed Parent-Child Contract

CONTRACT

I,____Paul____, agree to: *(1) Clean my gerbil's cage*

each Saturday. (2) Vacuum around the cage each

*Saturday.*_____

_____

We, Mother and Father, agree to: *Allow Paul to keep the*

gerbil in his bedroom. If cage and surrounding area aren't

cleaned each Saturday, then gerbil goes back to the

*garage.*_____

_____

Date contract begins: *June 13*_____

Date contract ends: *Contract continues as long as*

                          *gerbil is in Paul's room.*_____

Date contract signed: *June 13.*_____

Agreed to by: *Paul*_____
                         (Child's Signature)

                         *Mother*_____
                         (Mother)

                         *Father*_____
                         (Father)

Contracts help families by clarifying agreements and responsibilities. If Paul doesn't clean his gerbil's cage each week as agreed, then his gerbil must be returned to the garage.

Contracts have been used with adolescents to encourage regular attendance at school and to set a deadline for returning home after dates. Before your son or daughter begins using the family car, negotiate and sign a contract stating his or her responsibilities.

See Chapter 20 for examples of how a written agreement between child, teacher, and parent can improve a child's school progress or adjustment at school.

2. Negotiate a solution with your child. Try to jointly agree on a solution rather than forcing one on him. The older your child, the more real power or authority you should let him have in helping to figure out a solution. This means using your child's best ideas as well as your own. Don't impose a contract on an adolescent. If you do, he may rebel and intensify family conflict.

Be sure that your spouse stays involved throughout the negotiations. Sometimes, busy husbands or wives try to shift negotiating responsibilities to their spouses. Choose a time when everyone is relatively calm. Be patient, positive, and stay focused on the actual behavior or actions which you want to occur.

Before my family subscribed to cable television, we spent considerable time discussing potential problems and solutions. My wife and I were concerned that our boys would watch too much television or watch programs oriented toward sex and violence. After several weeks of negotiations, the four of us signed a contract. That contract later helped prevent a lot of family disagreements.

3. Write down the negotiated agreement. The contract should state what you agree to do and what your child agrees to do. Use clear and positive language so your child can understand the contract and also feel encouraged by it. State the consequences if the parties don't comply with the agreement. Include a date when the contract ends or is to be renegotiated.

The contract should be fair to all. Everyone should be gaining something as well as giving up something. It states what each person is to do and what he is to receive in return. Consider the contract which Mr. and Mrs. Carr negotiated with their son, Paul.

4. Sign the contract, post it, and follow through with your responsibilities. After everyone signs the contract, post it on a bulletin board or put it where everyone can find it. If your child says that a posted contract embarrasses him in front of his friends, post it in an inconspicuous place or keep the contract in a special folder. Save all old contracts in a folder called, "Family Contracts."

If your child doesn't fulfill his responsibilities, follow the consequences written into the contract. Most families who use contracts say they're great tools for preventing and solving problems.

Main Points To Remember:

- *Point-rewards* and *tokens* can motivate your child to improve a wide variety of problem behaviors.

- Your child can select tangible rewards and privileges from a *menu of rewards,* after earning points or tokens.

- *Parent-child contracts* help solve family problems, especially disagreements between parents and older children.

Chapter 15

Timing-Out Two Children

Fights between brothers and sisters are common problems which parents face.

When *two* children misbehave, it isn't always necessary to know who started the problem or who is mostly at fault. Just send both children to time-out in separate time-out places.

In this chapter, you'll learn why *timing-out two children* is an effective method for handling problems between children. You'll also learn when and how to use *time-out for two*. This method is most effective when used with children who are at least three or four years old.

Reducing Conflict *Between* Children

Time-Out For Two

Ten-year-old Andrew and nine-year-old Angela were making faces and calling each other names. Since father believed that Andrew had started the conflict, father placed only Andrew in time-out.

As Andrew was leaving time-out, father overheard another argument beginning between Andrew and his sister.

Angela: *"You had to go to time-out, Andrew! Ha, ha, ha! Dad is on my side, and he put you in time-out!"*

Andrew: *"Shut up! You know that you started calling me names first. Do you want to get a fat lip?"*

Angela: *"Ha! Just try it! You are a big baby, and you are always starting fights around here, and Mom and Dad know it!"*

At this moment father walks up, annoyed with both children.

Father: *"Time-out for fighting! Angela, you in the bathroom! Andrew — the back bedroom! Go!!"*

Good for father! He recognizes that it takes two to fight. Also he is beginning to realize that *time-out for two* is often more effective than correcting only *one* child or personally solving persistent problems between his children.

Name calling, threatening gestures, loud arguing, hostile teasing, kicking, and hitting are common behavior problems which parents face. By acting as a judge or referee, you might take too much responsibility for solving problems between your children. Too frequently, parents intervene and attempt to determine which child started the disagreement in order to blame and scold the guilty child. Consequently, the children become overly dependent on parents to settle problems rather than resolving their own conflicts. Also, the possibility always exists that the parent may "judge" incorrectly.

Many children delight in getting a brother or sister into trouble. A clever child may begin an argument, but make it appear as if the other child started the conflict. Sometimes, a younger child who appears helpless or innocent actually provokes an older child into harassing him. When children have disagreements and arguments, it's frequently difficult to say who started the conflict.

Children love getting attention from their parents. Your children may be learning to get considerable attention from you by constantly arguing and fussing with each other. Of course you dislike hearing and seeing conflict between your children. However, if you step in and handle the disagreement yourself, you may be "accidentally" rewarding one or both of your children for continuously arguing.

What should you do as a parent? When two children are arguing and fighting with each other, consider sending both children to time-out regardless of who started it.

There are three advantages for timing-out both children. First, you don't have to take sides or determine which child is mostly at fault. *Second,* you don't accidentally reward their fighting with lots of attention while you settle their arguments. *Third,* both children are discouraged from continuing their conflicts because both receive the same boring and unpleasant time-out experience.

When And How To Use *Time-Out For Two*

Time-out for two is effective for handling problems between two or more children as discussed above. Another appropriate time to use time-out for two is when your children get into trouble *together,* even though they may be getting along fine with each other. Let's assume that, despite several scoldings, your children continue chasing each other through the house, playing tag, and slamming doors. This would be a suitable time to place both children in time-out.

Time-Out For Four

One Saturday morning my son Eric, five years old, was playing inside with three neighborhood friends. Their playing became increasingly noisy and rough. They continued slamming doors and running in the house even though I had told them to stop.

Finally I said, *"Time-out for playing so rough! Eric, you in that corner. Elizabeth, in that corner! You Amy, there! And Jeff, you sit in that corner!"* Each child went to a different corner of the room and sat down. I set the timer for five minutes, their average age, and placed the timer in the middle of the room. These three neighborhood children had learned to comply with time-out because they knew that if they didn't, they would have to go home immediately.

After a couple of minutes the doorbell rang. It was Elizabeth's mother and she was looking for Elizabeth! I said, *"Elizabeth and the rest of the kids are in time-out for running in the house."* She said, *"What's time-out?"*

When I started to explain, the timer rang, the children left time-out, and Elizabeth walked up to her mother. As Elizabeth and her mother walked down the porch steps, I could hear five year old Elizabeth further explaining time-out to her mother.

Look over the list, *"Misbehavior Which Deserves Time-Out"* in Chapter 4, "What is Time-Out? When Do Parents Use It?" Time-out for two would be fitting for almost all of these behaviors if both children are involved in these misbehaviors together.

Prior to using time-out for two, you should be experienced in timing-out each of the children individually. Before actually placing two children in time-out, wait for the moment when both children are misbehaving.

Then immediately use the *Time-Out And 10 (words)-10 (seconds) Method.* Tell both of them to go to separate time-out places. Be sure that no one takes toys to time-out and that they can't see each other while in time-out. Place the timer where each child can hear it ring. Of course, more than two children may be timed-out if each has experienced time-out previously.

How long should the children be in time-out if they are, for example, six and ten years old? Set the timer for eight minutes since their average age is eight.

Be sure to give your children attention and special privileges when they behave and get along with each other. After experiencing a pleasant morning at home, one mother of two young children, said, *"You two are playing so well with each other this morning. Let's go to the park this afternoon! It's easy to go places together when you get along so well!"*

Main Points To Remember:
- Since it takes two to fight, consider using *time-out for two.*
- Use the Time-Out And 10 (words)-10 (seconds) Method to send two or more children to time-out. Send them to separate time-out places and set the timer for their average age.
- Timing-out two children has some distinct advantages over other methods of handling persistent problems between children.
- When your children are behaving themselves and getting along with each other, be sure to reward them with lots of attention and praise.

Chapter 16

Timing-Out A Toy
Instead Of The Child

PROBLEMS PARENTS FACE

"It's mine!"

"NO! IT'S MINE!"

Toys often cause problems between children. Sometimes children hit others with toys, damage furniture with toys, or refuse to share toys.

TIMING-OUT A TOY —
AN EFFECTIVE SOLUTION

"We better share next time. If we don't share, nobody will get to play with it again. Dad will put our toy back in time-out. . . ."

In the future, Jeffrey and Lisa will be less likely to fight over a toy. They will be more likely to share it. *Timing-out a toy* is an effective but gentle method for improving the behavior of children.

In this chapter I describe a useful variation of time-out called *timing-out a toy* instead of the child.* It's easy to follow the

---

See an interesting demonstration of *timing-out a toy* in a free video clip at www.sosprograms.com The video clip is called "Time-Out, Effective Use." The "toy" in this example is a TV set. The children are arguing over which TV program to watch.

*When you *time-out a toy* or another object your child briefly loses the privilege of playing with that object. This time-out procedure, which follows a child's misbehavior with the object, also can be called a *logical consequence*. Logical consequences are discussed in Chapter 5.

correct steps for using this effective method of discipline. Other skills discussed in this chapter include *using a timer to take turns* and placing personal belongings in a *Sunday Box* if they are left scattered about the house.

Timing-Out The Robot *Instead* Of The Children

Last night father enjoyed bringing home a toy robot for five-year-old Jeffrey and six-year-old Lisa. This morning he reluctantly spent most of his time deciding "who had the toy first," insisting that both children take turns, and scolding them for arguing with each other.

To stop the nearly continuous squabbling, father finally decided to put the toy robot in time-out. He placed the robot on top of the refrigerator, set the portable timer for ten minutes, and put the ticking timer next to the robot. He then turned to his children and said, *"After the timer rings, I will get the robot down for you. However, if you two continue to have problems sharing the toy, then it will go back into time-out!"*

The robot didn't have to go back to time-out that morning because Jeffrey and Lisa learned to share their new toy rather than having it put in time-out. They each learned that they would lose the fun of playing with their new toy if they continued fighting over it.

Timing-Out Toys And Stopping Misbehavior

Children spend an enormous amount of time playing with toys and other objects. Toys provide a way for children to socialize with other children and with their parents.

Consider *timing-out a toy* instead of using some other discipline method for helping your child to learn increased self-control. There are three situations when you might choose to time-out a toy rather than a child — (1) Your child misbehaves while playing with a toy (such as damaging furniture with a toy); (2) Two children argue and fuss over a toy rather than sharing it; and (3) Two children misbehave and their misbehavior involves a toy (playing catch with an expensive toy not intended to be thrown).

When your child invites a friend over to play, and the misbehavior of the two children involves a toy, you might consider timing-out the toy. The parents of the other child couldn't object to your placing a toy in time-out — although they might be puzzled by this procedure! For adults responsible for several children at one time, such as preschool teachers and day-care workers, timing-out a toy is an ideal method of discipline.

You may be wondering, why should parents time-out a toy instead of their child. A child who is in time-out loses the opportunity to learn new things and to try new behavior that might be rewarding or enjoyable. You don't want children spending too much time in time-out. Also, *when you use discipline, you should use the mildest form which is still effective in changing behavior.* Timing-out a toy is a milder correction than timing-out the child. Timing-out a toy gives you an effective alternative to timing-out your child and an additional way to back up your warnings.

When two children repeatedly fuss over a toy, don't be overly concerned with finding out which child is at fault or which child should be blamed for the argument. *Avoid taking sides.* Simply place the toy or object in time-out. That way neither child will be rewarded for arguing and fussing. Also, after the two "combatants" lose their toy to time-out, they will be more motivated in the future to work out their own problems.

Steps For Timing-Out Toys

How do you time-out a toy or another object? Use the *Time-Out And 10 (words)-10 (seconds) Method.* When your child misbehaves with a toy, quickly remove the toy and place it in time-out. Use no more than ten words and ten seconds before placing the toy in time-out. After timing-out the toy, tell your child why it had to go to time-out. Then ask him to state aloud why the object was placed in time-out. Be brief and avoid scolding.

Don't require your child to place a toy in time-out himself. You can do it much quicker and also avoid a possible power struggle. Always use a portable timer. It will signal your child when he may resume playing with a toy. The reasons for using a portable timer when timing-out toys are essentially the same as for timing-out children. Review "Reasons For Using A Portable Timer" in Chapter 10.

For children who are *two or three years old,* place the toy out of the child's reach and where it can easily be observed by you. Next, get the portable timer and set it for a short period of time, usually two to five minutes. Place the ticking timer next to the toy so that your child sees the toy and timer together. Then briefly tell him why the toy went to time-out. For example, say,

Timing-Out Toys And Other Objects:

A Solution To Persistent Problems —

Examples For Parents

Problem Behavior	A Solution*
1. Two sisters, ten and thirteen years old, continue squabbling about which television program to watch. They repeatedly complain to mother and want her to solve their problem.	1. Mother turns off the television, sets a timer for ten minutes, and places the timer on the television set. She should repeat this procedure if necessary.
2. Four-year-old Alan repeatedly rides his Big Wheel vehicle too near the street after being told not to do so by father.	2. Father puts the Big Wheel in a time-out place inside the garage for twenty minutes.
3. Six-year-old Andrea plays catch with her pet hamster.	3. The hamster is placed back in its cage and can't come out for the rest of the day.
4. Daniel and his friend, both four years old, knock over each other's blocks and threaten to throw them at each other.	4. Daniel's mother sets a timer for ten minutes and places it next to the pile of building blocks. Mother also explains time-out to Daniel's surprised friend.
5. Erin repeatedly complains that her brother won't take turns with their new video game.	5. Father turns off the video game and sets the timer for ten minutes. He may need to repeat this procedure a couple of times.
6. The stereo in the living room is vibrating the apartment again.	6. The stereo is turned off, and the portable timer is set for fifteen minutes and placed on the stereo.

*Parents, of course, must decide which behavior problems are serious enough to warrant a mild correction such as timing-out a toy. There are ways of handling the above problems other than using time-out. However, timing-out a toy is quick, effective, and easy for parents to use.

You hit the coffee table with your toy. That is why I put it in time-out." Next, tell him that the toy can leave time-out as soon as the timer rings. When the timer rings, again briefly tell him why the toy had to go to time-out and then hand it to him. Don't ask him to apologize for his bad behavior or make him promise to be good in the future.

For children who are *four and older,* it's usually not necessary to place the toy out of the child's reach. Simply say, *"Time-out for* (give the name of object)! *Don't touch it!"* Get the timer, set it for ten to fifteen minutes, and place the timer next to the toy. Then tell your child why you placed the toy in time-out. Tell him that he may retrieve the toy from time-out after he hears the timer ring. No one touches a ticking timer or an object in time-out. If they do, then they get to go to time-out themselves! Even impulsive children quickly learn to control themselves and to wait for the timer to ring before removing a toy from time-out.

More Ideas For Parents

- *Practice taking turns using a timer*

- *Sunday Box*

- *Distraction*, for preschoolers

Help your children to *practice taking turns by using a timer.* Timers keep accurate track of the time and are fair to each child.

For example, if your two children have trouble sharing a new video game, sit down with them and have them practice the desirable behavior (taking turns). Have each child set the timer for five minutes and play the video game until the timer rings. Then, the child playing the game immediately must give up the game and hand it to the other child. The other child sets the timer for five minutes and begins his turn.

Continue helping them to practice setting the timer and taking turns until you are sure both children know the procedure. If they choose, however, to continue squabbling over the video game rather than sharing it, place the video game in time-out. This will motivate each of them to cooperate.

It's often difficult to get children to pick up their toys, shoes, clothes, records, and other objects which they leave on the floor and scattered about the house. Use a "*Sunday Box*" for out-of-place personal belongings.

Place a cardboard box, marked *Sunday Box*, in the living room or in any other room which you want cleared of clutter. Set a timer for ten minutes and place it next to the box. Then announce to your family that you are putting all out-of-place belongings in the box when the timer rings. The objects are kept there until Sunday, when you release them to their owners. Give no further warning and do not scold. After the timer rings, pick up all out-of-place objects, place them in the box, and place the box in a closet. No one touches the objects or the Sunday Box until Sunday. After losing their toys and other objects several times, children will pick up their own belongings and you won't have to scold and nag.

When you see two toddlers or preschoolers arguing and fussing over a toy, consider using *distraction*. Draw their attention or redirect their interest to a new toy or activity. One or both children will usually give up the old toy or activity and try the new activity. Consequently, they have another opportunity to play cooperatively or apart from each other. Most young children can be easily distracted.

When your child plays well with others, reward him with your praise, approval, and attention. Young children need lots of *encouragement*, and they love words of *praise* for good behavior.

Main Points To Remember:

- When your child's misbehavior involves a toy, use the *Time-Out And 10 words-10 seconds Method* for placing the toy in time-out.

- *Timing-out toys* and other objects gives you an effective alternative to timing-out your child.

- Help your children *practice setting the timer and taking turns* with a toy or activity.

- Use a *Sunday Box* for out-of-place toys and other belongings.

Chapter 17

Handling Aggressive And Dangerous Behavior

"Help! Help!"

Stop dangerous behavior immediately. After stopping the behavior, use several methods of effective discipline.

"I Was Just Going To Scare Him With It!"

Early one Saturday morning, while organizing my garage, I heard two desperate cries, *"Help! Help!"* My five-year-old son, Eric, was holding a bat and chasing Jeff, our six-year-old neighbor. Jeff was obviously terrified and "running for his life." Considering the situation, Jeff's emotional state and behavior were appropriate!

Running out the garage door, I shouted, *"Stop swinging that bat! No hitting!"* I caught up with Eric and grabbed the bat, saying, *"Don't ever chase anyone with a bat! That's very dangerous!"* Next, I said, *"Time-out! Go sit on those porch steps, NOW!"* Eric walked off to time-out.

I turned to check on Jeff, but he had disappeared, apparently running off to "safety." Next, I looked at the bat and was somewhat relieved to find that it was a hollow plastic bat used for hitting plastic balls.

After Eric's time-out was over, we had the following talk:

Father: *"Eric, never try to hit someone with a bat or with any object! It's dangerous and will hurt someone badly."*

Eric: *"I wasn't really going to hit Jeff with the bat. I was just going to scare him with it!"*

Father: *"Never use an object for hitting or scaring someone! Eric, tell me again. What did you do that was dangerous?"*

Eric: *"I chased Jeff with a bat. He wouldn't take turns hitting the ball."*

Father: *"Chasing Jeff with a bat was dangerous and wrong. Tell me, what can you do next time if Jeff won't take turns, and you get mad? What can you do that is safe? You tell me."*

Eric: *"Well, I could tell him that I won't play with him if he doesn't take turns. . . . I could tell his mother on him. . . . I could come and tell you that he won't take turns."*

Father: *"Those are good, safe things to do if someone won't take turns. I am really proud that you thought of these safer ways of behaving in the future.*

Eric and I continued discussing his behavior and feelings. I also put the bat up for one week, a mild logical consequence for threatening someone with it.

There are many motives for aggressive behavior. A child may try to hurt another person because he is angry and upset, because he wants to get his way, or because he wants to dominate and control the other person. He might want to impress other kids. As parents, however, we must stop behavior which threatens or hurts others. Aggressive children run a high risk of being maladjusted as teenagers and as adults.

A child might also endanger *himself* by disobeying important safety rules or by taking serious risks. For example, a child might ride his tricycle into a busy street, play with matches, or go too near dangerous equipment.

Perched On The Overpass

Nine-year-old Brandi and her father walked through a large city park. Brandi was especially difficult to handle that afternoon and ran ahead of her father, nearly getting lost several times. Dad continued to nag and shout, and Brandi continued to "do her own thing."

As they approached the edge of the park, Brandi darted ahead and disappeared along the curving sidewalk. Dad finally caught up, and found her perched on the edge of a tall pedestrian overpass, casually looking down on four lanes of traffic moving below her!

He tried to remain calm as he told Brandi to slowly get down. Then he scolded her and also gave her a nine-minute time-out under a large tree back in the park. For the rest of their walk, Brandi had to stay within ten feet of him or she got another *immediate time-out.* Brandi quickly became manageable.

Managing Aggressive And Dangerous Behavior

You have two goals for managing aggressive and dangerous behavior. Your first goal is to immediately stop the misbehavior in order to protect your child or others. Your second goal is to effectively handle the misbehavior so that it won't occur again. *In order to meet these two goals, keep in mind the following basic steps.*

A. Stop the behavior, deliver a brief scolding, and name the unacceptable behavior. You sometimes need to immediately step in and restrain your child when he is behaving aggressively or dangerously. There is a time for talk and there is a time for action! Act quickly when the safety of your child or other children is in question.

After stopping the dangerous behavior, deliver a brief, harsh scolding and name the particular misbehavior. Don't enter into an argument or discussion before sending him to time-out. In a loud, firm voice, say, *"No! You are never to . . .* (name the aggressive or dangerous action)! I emphatically and explicitly told Eric, *"Don't ever chase anyone with a bat!"*

B. Place your child in time-out immediately. When correcting aggressive or dangerous behavior, it's time for an immediate time-out and not time for talk. You can talk later.

Quickly send your child to time-out after stopping his dangerous behavior. Don't skip this important step and do use a timer!

You may be wondering, *"Will an aggressive child cooperate by going to time-out?"* The answer is, "YES!" Chapter 12 tells how to get a rebellious child to cooperate with the time-out method of discipline.

If both of your children are involved in serious misbehavior and if both are "guilty" to some extent, use "time-out for two." When you use time-out for two you don't have to know who is guilty or most guilty. Timing-out two children is discussed in Chapter 15.

While your child is in time-out, prepare yourself for the "after time-out" discussion. Mentally rehearse what you are going to say. Think about *why* your child may have behaved dangerously or impulsively.

C. Talk to him about his aggressive or dangerous behavior. The time to talk is after time-out is over. Tell your child again what he did that was aggressive or dangerous. Tell him why his behavior was unacceptable. Then ask him to tell you, in his own words, what he did that was dangerous. At this point, you are not asking him to apologize or promise not to do it again. You are merely asking him to *describe* what he did. In the discussion with my son, I said, *"Eric, tell me again. What did you do that was dangerous?"*

After he describes his aggressive or dangerous behavior, ask him to describe several alternative ways of safely behaving in the future. When talking with Eric, I said, *"Tell me, what can you do next time if Jeff won't take turns and you get mad? What can you do that is safe?"*

After your child tells you about alternative, safer ways of behaving, give him your praise. Encourage his ideas. Help him discover alternative ways to cope with difficult people and solve problems in the future. Five-year-old Eric told me about several things he might do the next time that Jeff refused to take turns — *"I could tell him that I won't play with him if he doesn't take turns. . . . I could tell his mother on him. . . . I could come and tell you that he won't take turns."*

If your child can't think of any alternative, safer ways of behaving, then you should help him determine some alternatives. If he angrily "clams up" and refuses to talk to you, wait until later to talk, or consider sending him to time-out once more, but only once more. Following this second time-out, again attempt to discuss alternative, safer ways of behaving.

Basic Steps For Handling Aggressive Or Dangerous Behavior — Parent's Check List

Immediate Steps To Follow:

___ 1. Stop the behavior.

___ 2. Deliver a brief scolding and name the unacceptable behavior.

___ 3. Place him in time-out immediately.

After Time-Out Is Over:

___ 4. Ask him to say what he did that was aggressive or dangerous.

___ 5. Help him describe one or two other ways of behaving safely or nonaggressively in the future. Reward him with your praise after he tells you about these safer ways   of behaving.

___ 6. Follow through with a mild logical consequence or behavior penalty. (See Chapter 5)

___ 7. Use reflective listening *if* your child is in the mood to talk. (Chapter 18)

D. Follow though with a mild logical consequence or behavior penalty. Logical consequences and behavior penalties are described in Chapter 5. If your child is small and acts physically aggressive toward the neighborhood bully, he will probably receive a *natural consequence,* such as a black eye or other bruises!

If your son or daughter uses a toy or object when behaving

in a dangerous or aggressive way, consider also *timing-out the toy* or object for an extended period of time. Eric lost the use of his plastic bat for one week.

Twelve-year-old Mary enjoyed frightening younger children by riding her bicycle at high speed and then swerving to miss them. She permanently stopped this dangerous behavior after her mother locked up her bicycle for two weeks.

After Brandi's father found her perched on the overpass, he made her stay within ten feet of him for the rest of their walk that afternoon. This brief *restriction* was a logical consequence for her prior dangerous behavior.

E. Use reflective listening if your child is in the mood to talk. After time-out is over, guess out loud at what your child was feeling at the time she behaved dangerously. Then ask her if she had this feeling. The next chapter shows how to use "reflective listening" so that you can help your child to express her feelings. Children who understand their feelings, and know how to express their anger and frustration with words, have greater control over their aggressive, impulsive behavior.

More Help For The Aggressive Child

Aggressive children maintain a high rate of verbally and physically aggressive behavior toward family members, other children, adults (including teachers), and property. These children are quick to hit, push, kick, bite, spit, tease, torment, intimidate, have a tantrum, throw things, and cry. Many children *occasionally* engage in some of these behaviors, but the aggressive child *frequently* engages in *many* of these behaviors.

Although his aggression is an almost "automatic" response to stress and frustration, it also has a purpose. *His aggression forces or coerces others to give him what he wants.* When others resist giving in to his demands or attempt to correct his aggressive behavior, the aggressive child usually responds by becoming increasingly belligerent and "out-of-control." Getting out-of-control is one way aggressive children attempt to control others. Aggressive children also are more likely to lie and deny responsibility for their actions.

Aggression can lead to grave consequences. Another family counselor and I worked with nine-year-old Steven and his family. Steven's parents and the court sought help for him after he impulsively picked up a pipe and, in a fit of anger, struck and killed another child. Don't postpone trying to correct a child's aggressive pattern of behavior.

The aggressive child is usually *noncompliant*. That is, he doesn't comply with requests from his parents and other adults — he doesn't mind and obey as well as other children. His temper tantrum is a means of "training parents" to stop asking him to do things he doesn't want to do. Also, his tantrum prevents others from interfering with what he does want to do.

PROBLEMS PARENTS FACE

"All I did was ask her to take out the trash. I guess that she doesn't want to do it!"

The aggressive child often has temper tantrums when told to do things that she doesn't want to do.

It's difficult to help the aggressive child — or even like him. He can keep a family or an entire classroom in angry turmoil. Parents and teachers who try to help the aggressive child often have a lot of difficulty dealing with their own feelings of anger and frustration toward the child.

Many parents with an angry, out-of-control child secretly hope that a hidden inner cause for their child's aggressive behavior can be found. They also want to believe that they can *send* their child to a counselor who will discover an "inner problem" and fix their child's personality and behavior by using a new, powerful method of therapy. Parents at the other extreme feel helpless and believe that nothing can be done to help their son or daughter.

The truth is that the aggressive child can be helped and

sometimes dramatically changed. However, helping the aggressive child requires much from parents. It requires hard work, patience, "follow-through," caring, and the consistent application of the SOS child management methods described in this book. Professional help is often necessary as well. Chapter 22 discusses when and how to get professional help.

When the aggressive child *acts* aggressively and dangerously toward others, consistently follow the "Basic Steps For Handling Aggressive Or Dangerous Behavior" described earlier. Every time that he makes verbal or physical threats, simply use time-out or another method of mild correction such as a logical consequence or behavior penalty.

Be sure to reward the aggressive child with attention and praise when he behaves nonaggressively and when he minds. Also, consider beginning a point-reward program to help him improve his behavior, as described in Chapter 14. Allow him to earn points for each half-day that he is free of aggressive behavior. After earning points, he trades them for material and activity rewards.

Many children who are aggressive at home are also aggressive at school. Coordinate your efforts to reduce your child's aggressive behavior with the efforts of his teacher. Study Chapter 19 to learn how to work effectively with your child's teacher. Reducing aggression requires a coordinated "attack"!

Aggressive, violent behavior is becoming increasingly common in The United States. Our homicide rate is seven times higher than in England, Europe, Japan and in many other developed countries. Our children are exposed to considerable violence and sexualized violence in popular media and entertainment programs. Popular heroes in the media frequently solve problems with crude language, aggression and violence.

Children often increase their aggressive behavior by being exposed to "models" who act aggressively. As mentioned in earlier chapters, be sure that you and your spouse are good models. Greatly limit your child's exposure to aggressive models in movies, television, music, computer games, some televised sports such as wrestling, and printed materials.

Main Points To Remember:
- Use the "Basic Steps For Handling Aggressive or Dangerous Behavior" whenever you see that behavior occur.
- Limit your child's exposure to aggressive peers and models in cartoons, movies, TV shows, and popular music.
- You can help the *aggressive child* to improve his behavior by using SOS child management methods.

Chapter 18

Helping Your Child
Express Feelings

"They said that you couldn't play with them because you are a girl? . . . I can see why you feel hurt and angry. . . ."

"No Girls Allowed!"

Relaxing in his easy chair, father jumped when ten-year-old Stacy slammed the front door and stomped into the room. Wearing a baseball cap, glove, and an angry scowl, she said, *"Next time I am going to use my bat on those boys!"*

Father: *"What happened, Stacy? Tell me about it."*

Stacy: *"I went out to play ball, and those mean boys wouldn't let me play!"*

Father: *"They wouldn't let you play?"*

Stacy: *"No! They said, 'No girls allowed,' and then they all laughed at me!"*

Father: *"They said that you couldn't play with them because you are a girl? . . . I can see why you feel hurt and angry. . . ."*

Stacy: *"Yes, they made me mad! And they hurt my feelings, too. I thought they were my friends."*

Father gave Stacy emotional support by being concerned, listening, and reflecting her feelings. He helped her realize that she was feeling more than just anger. She was also feeling hurt and rejected.

We want to protect our children from disappointments, frustrations, and conflicts with other people. However, we can't constantly keep them under our protective wing. What we can do is help them understand and cope with their feelings involving unpleasant experiences. By using *reflective listening,* we encourage our children to express and share feelings with us. *Reflective listening is briefly summarizing and restating to your child both her feelings and the situation that seems to have caused those feelings.**

By sharing unpleasant feelings with you, your child will be less hurt or burdened by them. She'll also gain increased control over her emotions and behavior, and will make better choices in meeting the challenges and disappointments of daily living. Communication with your child will improve, and you'll have a closer relationship.

How early should parents begin reflective listening? Three-year-olds aren't too young to benefit if parents are brief and use simple words. Boys need help in expressing feelings as much as girls. Boys and girls who are in touch with their own feelings become better adjusted men and women.

Use Basic Skills Of Reflective Listening

Use the communication skill of reflective listening to help your child learn to express her feelings. *Follow five guidelines when your child begins to share her feelings with you:*

---

*Reflective listening is also called "active listening."

1. Accept and respect all of your child's feelings. Do this by listening quietly and attentively and being nonjudgemental. Of course you needn't accept all of her *actions or behaviors*, just her feelings. She can tell you how angry she is at her brother, but she isn't permitted to express her anger by teasing or hitting him.

2. Show her that you are listening to what she says. Your close attention rewards her for expressing her ideas and feelings to you. Stop what you are doing, turn toward her, maintain eye contact, and listen carefully. Also, show her your attention by nodding your head and by an occasional, *"Um hum . . . yes . . . Mmm . . ."*

3. Tell your child what you hear her saying and what you think she is feeling. Occasionally summarize, restate, or rephrase the core of what she tells you — *both her feelings and the situation that seems to have caused her feelings.** It's not enough to only listen and understand. *You must also reflect back to her, with words, what she is saying, thinking, and feeling.* This is *reflective listening* — a skill which takes practice to develop.

Try not to repeat your daughter's *exact words*. Use *similar words* that capture the same meaning and feeling. Say to your disappointed three-year-old, *"You feel bad* (the feeling) *because you couldn't go to the store with Daddy this time* (the situation)."

Your child may say things which you find terribly upsetting or threatening. For example, she may say, *"No one at school likes me!"* Brace yourself and don't be swept away by a flood of concern or guilt as you listen and reflect what she says. Be a helpful parent and encourage her to express whatever she feels. She needs your help. By being an effective sounding board and mirror for your child, you are helping her to cope with her feelings and to make better choices for herself.

Children often exaggerate both their negative feelings and the distasteful situation behind those feelings. Help your child understand and clarify her feelings and her description of the situation by using reflective listening. However, don't tell her that she is exaggerating because this will make her less willing to share other feelings with you.

---

*Unpleasant situations and events do influence our feelings. However, what a person tells himself about these events (that is, silent self-talk statements) has a greater influence on his feelings. In *SOS Help For Emotions* book, I describe how beliefs and self-talk primarily cause our feelings and behavior. Also, I describe the steps for improving one's feelings by correcting one's faulty self-talk. This book, based on cognitive therapy, is suitable for helping both adults and adolescents. See ordering information at the end of this book.

4. Give her feelings a name. Labeling feelings is the first step to understanding and managing them. Look over the two lists of feelings, "Names For Pleasant Feelings" and "Names For Unpleasant Feelings." These two lists give labels for common positive and negative feelings experienced by both children and adults. If your child is young, be sure to use simple words when you help label her feelings.

After listening carefully to what she says and watching her facial expressions, make an "educated guess" and tentatively label her feelings. For example, say to your nine-year-old, *"You seem to be feeling disappointed (a feeling) or perhaps a little resentful (another feeling) because of the way your teacher treated you (the situation)."* If you are incorrect with your first guess, then try again. Be respectful, calm, and maintain a slow pace in what you say. Encourage her to tell you if your guess is wrong and to help you correct your guess.

NAMES FOR PLEASANT FEELINGS

SOS

accepted, liked	glad
appreciated	good, great
capable, confident	grateful, thankful
successful	pleased
comfortable, relaxed	love, loved
eager	satisfied, happy
cheerful, elated	enjoy, like
hopeful, optimistic	proud
encouraged	respected
relieved	secure, safe

NAMES FOR UNPLEASANT FEELINGS

angry, mad	unhappy, miserable
resentful, want to get even	messed over, unfair
irritable, grumpy	unloved, neglected
scared, afraid	discouraged
disappointed, let down	embarrassed
lonely, left out	hurt
without a friend, rejected	tired
worthless, no good	bored
stupid, dumb	confused
upset, tense	frustrated
worried, anxious	inferior
insecure	guilty

5. Offer advice, suggestions, reassurance, or alternative ways of looking at the situation, only AFTER you help your child to examine how she feels. Advice, suggestions, and reassurance, if given first, will hamper your child's effort to express and understand her feelings.

How do you begin learning the skill of reflective listening? The technique for reflecting positive feelings is the same as for reflecting negative feelings. Most parents find it easier and more pleasant to practice the skill of reflective listening by beginning with their child's pleasant, positive feelings.

The next time your child tells you something and seems to have positive feelings (such as feeling excited, relieved, eager, proud, or happy) reflect these feelings. Also, reflect her description of the situation or event that seems to have caused the feelings. For example, say, *"You seem to feel relieved* (the feeling) *because your piano recital was cancelled* (the situation)." Or say, *"Getting invited to Mike's party* (the situation) *has sure made you feel excited and happy* (the feeling)." Practice the skill of reflective listening in order to learn it.

"I Feel Like I Don't Have A Friend Anymore"

When my oldest son, Eric, was four, I found him crying by our swing set in the back yard. Tears were streaming down through the dirt covering his face. Sobbing, he said, *"I hate Jeff! He threw dirt in my face!"* I tried to reflect his feelings by saying, *"You're mad at Jeff for throwing dirt, and also he hurt your feelings."* He replied, *"Yes, I feel like I don't have a friend anymore!"*

We walked to the house and I helped wash off the dirt. More importantly, I helped him cope with an insult from a friend by simply reflecting his feelings of anger and hurt. Later that afternoon, I watched Eric and Jeff happily playing together.

Reflective Listening And Problems Parents Face

Several problems may arise when your child expresses feelings to you. You can manage each of these problems.

Problem A — Your child expresses unpleasant feelings toward you. She may say, *"You won't let me go to the movies Friday night, and I'm mad at you!"* Allow her to express negative feelings toward you, but don't permit her to verbally abuse you. Don't allow her to call you names, swear at you, threaten, or have a screaming tantrum. Tell her that she may express her feelings, but that you won't tolerate verbal abuse. If she continues calling you names or screaming, consider leaving the room or using a mild correction.

Children must learn to recognize their feelings and to express their feelings without being aggressive, obnoxious, or verbally abusive. Also, when you express your feelings toward your child, be sure that you follow the rules too, and don't verbally abuse him or her. Be a good role model!

Problem B — You help your child to talk about her feelings. However, she continues feeling miserable or voices irrational plans. Even after you have listened carefully, given her useful suggestions, and mentioned the possible consequences of her actions, twelve-year-old Laura may still be unreasonable. She may walk away saying, *"My English teacher is mean and unfair and I hate her! But I'm going to show her. She'll be sorry. I going to keep whispering in class and I'm going to hand in my report late!"* Often we can't directly change our child's irrational feelings and choices. Laura may have to learn to improve her behavior through natural consequences — *The School of Hard Knocks.* That is, she may continue having to stay late after school for whispering in class, and she may get an "F" on that late report.

Problem C — Your child is critical of your attempts at reflective listening. Consider the following discussion between mother and ten-year-old Bradley. Even though mother is accurate and effective when using reflective listening, Bradley temporarily becomes annoyed with her. Mother, however, appropriately continues with her reflective listening skills.

> Bradley: *"I'm mad at Chad's parents. They won't let him do anything. They're always afraid he'll get hurt. They treat him like a baby."*

> Mother: *"You're saying that you are annoyed at his parents because they baby him?"*

> Bradley: *"That's what I said! There you go again, repeating what I say!"*

> Mother: *"Well, Bradley, I am interested in your thoughts about Chad and his parents."*

> Bradley: *"OK. One way that they baby him is not letting him go with me to . . . ."*

In addition, your child may say that you misunderstood his feelings. Later, however, you may discover that you correctly understood his feelings after all.

If your child remarks on your reflective listening, simply "keep your cool" and tell him that you are "concerned about his feelings and thoughts." Don't let your child's occasional negative reaction toward your reflective listening skills keep you from using these skills.

Enhance Your Child's Emotional Intelligence

What is emotional intelligence? Emotional intelligence is your child's ability to understand and manage emotions and behavior. Since your child's emotional intelligence is learned rather than inherited, it can be improved. Your effective use of SOS methods will improve your child's behavioral adjustment, emotional adjustment, resiliency, and emotional intelligence.

As your child grows older, help to develop the following five skills.

Five Emotional Intelligence Abilities

> • Knowing and labeling her emotions
>
> • Managing and soothing her emotions
>
> • Recognizing emotions in others
>
> • Managing relationships with others
>
> • Motivating herself to achieve her goals

Children who know their feelings are better able to manage them. Children who know and manage their feelings are better able to recognize the feelings of others and to manage relationships with others. That's why it's important for you to practice your reflective listening skills with your child. By helping her to know her feelings and emotions, you will be helping her to increase her emotional intelligence.

Learn more about developing your emotional intelligence and helping your child develop emotional intelligence by reading and using *SOS Help For Emotions.* More information about *SOS Help For Emotions: Managing Anxiety, Anger, And Depression* is at the end of this book. Also, you may read chapters from this book at www.sosprograms.com

Your son pays particularly close attention to you when you are frustrated with a problem or having a conflict with another person. By watching you, he is learning how he might handle his own emotions, frustrations, and conflicts with others in the future. Be a good role model!

Main Points To Remember:

- Helping your child to label her feelings is the first step to helping her to understand and manage them.

- *Reflective listening is summarizing and restating to your child, both his feelings and the situation that seems to have caused those feelings.*

- Use reflective listening to help your child label, understand, and cope with his feelings.

- Practice helping your child by reflecting both his pleasant and unpleasant feelings.

- Reflective listening helps children gain increased control over their emotions and behavior.

- Use SOS to enhance your child's emotional intelligence.

- When you are upset, be a good role model for your child.

Chapter 19

More Problem Behaviors — Questions And Solutions

"Always in motion! Is this normal for a six-year-old?"

In this chapter, we'll look at a variety of common childhood problems such as Attention-Deficit/Hyperactivity Disorder (ADHD), learning disorders, bedwetting, daytime enuresis, resisting chores, and bedtime problems. You'll learn more methods and skills for helping your child, including *racing the timer, grounding,* and the *resting chair.* Also, you'll discover additional ways for using *point-rewards.* Let's look at questions parents frequently ask.

Q: *"My six-year-old son, Jeremy, is very active, always in motion, and doesn't pay attention when I tell him things. His first grade teacher says that he might have ADHD. How can I tell if Jeremy has ADHD and, if so, what can I do to help him?"*

A: ADHD refers to Attention-Deficit/Hyperactivity Disorder. Most children with ADHD are persistently overactive, inattentive, impulsive, easily distractible, and have a short attention span when compared with other children of the same age. Many ADHD children experience school learning problems, have difficulty in getting along with peers, and are aggressive. ADHD is about seven times more common in boys than in girls. Parents and teachers usually report feeling frustrated and worn-out as they try to keep up with children who have ADHD. A similar term often used is ADD or Attention Deficit Disorder.

PROBLEMS PSYCHOLOGISTS FACE —
WHEN EVALUATING *ADHD* CHILDREN

"Why is he messing up my things? Who is in charge here anyway?"

To determine if Jeremy has ADHD or ADD, have him examined by a pediatrician and evaluated by a psychologist. The psychologist will want to talk with you and Jeremy's teacher as well. It's particularly important to give him lots of praise for completing an activity or chore. All SOS methods are especially appropriate for helping children with ADHD. Your pediatrician and psychologist will give you additional recommendations if they feel that Jeremy needs special help. Be sure to make an organized home environment. A disorganized home is especially disorganizing to ADHD kids.

Q: *"My six-year-old daughter dawdles when straightening her room, dressing for school, and going to bed. Is there any way that I can help her to speed up?"*

A: To speed up your daughter's slow behavior, try a helpful method called *racing the timer*. Set a portable kitchen timer for a reasonable period of time and reward her if she completes a task before the timer rings. For example, the next time that you announce it's bedtime, set a timer for 30 or 40 minutes. Tell her that she gets a bedtime story and a point on the point-reward calendar if she beats the timer. To beat the timer, she must put on her pajamas, brush her teeth, and be in bed when the timer rings.

Don't nag her to hurry and don't scold her if she loses the race. When she beats the timer, however, give her praise, a point on the calendar, and a bedtime story.

Five Ways Portable Timers Help Children

1. Timers can time-out one child.

2. Timers can time-out two children.

3. Timers can time-out toys involved in misbehavior.

4. Timers can help children take turns.

5. Children can race timers to speed up slow behavior.

Q: *"Are there more ways that timers may be used to help children?"*

A: There are five ways that portable timers can help improve behavior. Timers can *time-out one child, two or more children, or toys* that are involved in misbehavior. A timer can *help children take turns* when they want to play with the same toy, such as a video game. As mentioned, children can *race the timer* to speed up slow behavior. Timers are parent savers because they are easy to use, effective in changing behavior, and save wear and tear on parents. Timers are also child savers because they save children from having to listen to their parents nag and lecture them.

Q: *"Occasionally, our twelve-year-old daughter gets in a bad mood, is grumpy, grouchy, complains about everything, criticizes her younger sister, and says annoying things to the rest of the family. Should I send her to her room for this unpleasant behavior?"*

A: Yes, but first try *reflective listening* to determine what may be bothering her. Reflective listening is described in Chapter 18, "Helping Your Child Express Feelings." Perhaps nothing specific is troubling your daughter. Being grouchy with her family may just be a bad habit. Tell her that you understand that she feels grumpy. She has a right to her feelings, but she shouldn't subject the family to abusive behavior. Don't call it time-out, but *send her to her room.* Tell her that she may come out when she can stop grumbling, complaining, and criticizing her sister. Don't tell her how long to stay in her room. She decides when to come out. Fatigue sometimes causes grumpiness. If your daughter is grouchy because she is tired, she might decide to take a short nap before rejoining the family.

Q: *"My sixteen-month-old gets into everything and runs me ragged. What should I do?"*

A: SOS isn't responsible for children under two years of age, just for children two to twelve!

Q: *"My seven- and ten-year-old children avoid helping my husband and me when we wash the car, rake leaves, or do dishes. They often say that they feel sick or tired or that they don't want to help. Are there any more methods which encourage children to help parents with work?"*

A: A *resting chair* will encourage your child to help you with chores! This is the plan: Everyone who begins a chore works until it is completed — all the leaves are raked. If someone says they are too sick or too tired to help the family, then that person must sit on the resting chair. The resting chair doesn't have to be an actual chair. If you are working outdoors, a spot under a particular tree will do fine. Be sure that the place is near another family member who is working. The spot should be as dull, boring, and free of interesting objects as possible. The person who is working serves as a good model for the child who is resting!

A truly tired child — or adult — welcomes the opportunity to rest. However, if your child is pretending to be tired, he will soon get bored sitting in the resting chair and watching others. Most children will decide to leave the resting chair and help others with chores because they prefer some kind of activity to inactivity. Don't scold your child for sitting on the resting chair rather than working. Be sure that he doesn't get attention, talk on the phone, play with toys, or leave the chair except to help others finish the job. A resting chair is boring, and boredom helps motivate children to work! After your children help with chores, be sure to tell them that you appreciate their hard work.

Q: *"My nine-year-old son, Brandon, still wets the bed at night. I've heard that an alarm for bedwetting can help children to have dry nights. Could such an alarm help my son?"*

A: Yes! Bedwetting alarms can help children six and older to attain dry nights. Most children stop nighttime enuresis — wetting the bed — by the age of five or six. If they don't, they might need special help from their parents.

First, take Brandon to your pediatrician to be sure a medical problem isn't causing his bedwetting. Next, begin a special program to help Brandon. Follow these steps:

Step 1. Use a *"point-reward calendar for improving one behavior,"* as described in Chapter 14. The desired target behavior is dry nights, and Brandon should get a point for each dry night. When he accumulates enough points, he selects a reward from a *menu of rewards*.

Also, give him a lot of praise for each dry night. Never scold or shame him for wetting the bed!

Undoubtedly, he already feels embarrassed or humiliated because of his problem.

Step 2. Whenever Brandon discovers that he wet the bed, he is to immediately shower or bathe, and then place his wet sheets in the washer. This is a mild logical consequence for wetting his bed. Younger children need help from a parent in stripping a bed and drawing bath water. Steps one and two are often sufficient to help many children to completely stop wetting the bed within one or two months. However, if Brandon persists in bedwetting, continue with these two steps and begin step three.

Step 3. Purchase a *bedwetting alarm* from the internet after searching for "bedwetting alarms." The child wears a wetness sensor on his underpants which senses moisture and activates a battery alarm. Expect to pay about $90 for an effective alarm of good quality. The best alarm that I have seen is a Malem Ultimate 1 bedwetting alarm. It has been available at www.bedwettingstore.com

Since it takes only two seconds for the alarm to sound, Brandon will get instant feedback that he wet the bed. He will learn to correct his bedwetting by conditioning. He may need to use the alarm for a couple of months before he overcomes the problem.

An alarm is extremely effective in helping children and adolescents to stop wetting the bed. However, if you purchase an alarm, also continue following steps one and two. After attaining dry nights, your child might return to bedwetting. Don't despair. Simply follow the steps again. Most children don't return to bedwetting after a second time through the program.

If you correctly follow all three steps and your son or daughter persists in bedwetting, you may wish to consult your pediatrician, a psychologist, or another behavioral specialist for additional help.

Q: *"What help do you recommend for children who wet on themselves during the day, after they are toilet trained?"*

A: A child who is five or older and toilet trained may slip back into occasional daytime enuresis. Try the following program:

Each day that your child is dry, give her three points on the *point-reward calendar*. If her problem is more frequent than once a day, then divide the day into morning, afternoon, and evening. Give her a point for each part of the day that she is accident free. She can earn up to three points a day!

Encourage her to exchange her points for an item on the *reward menu* as soon as she earns enough points. Also, at the end of each day compliment her if she hasn't had any accidents that day.

Never scold her for having an accident. Instead, have her immediately bathe, put on fresh clothes, and rinse out the soiled clothes herself.

Q: *"My neighbors tell me that they restrict or 'ground' their thirteen-year-old son for two or three weeks when he breaks rules. What is grounding, and do you recommend it as a method of discipline? I am thinking about using it with my teenage daughter."*

A: *Grounding is briefly restricting a child or adolescent to her home as a consequence for bad behavior.* She isn't permitted to visit friends or to go places without her parents as she normally does. When used correctly, grounding can help preadolescents and teenagers to improve their behavior.

If you use grounding, be sure that you follow two rules. Tell you child in advance what misbehavior will cause grounding. Also, always keep the duration of grounding short — usually not more than a weekend or one week. Grounding a teenager for a period of two or three weeks is overly severe and is not effective for improving behavior.

Q: *"My nine-year-old daughter, April, earns poor grades in school. Her teacher says that she may have a 'learning disorder.' What is a 'learning disorder' and what should I do next in order to help my daughter?"*

A: A learning disorder (also called a learning disability or LD) means that a child's achievement in reading, arithmetic, or written expression of ideas is significantly below her age and level of intelligence. Your daughter should be evaluated by a pediatrician and an eye doctor who are interested in school learning problems. It's also essential that a psychologist talk to you and your daughter and obtain measures of her intellectual capacity and educational skills. Be sure to follow the recommendations of the pediatrician and psychologist.

Also look in the Index — 46 Problem Behaviors And 23 SOS Methods. Forty-six problem behaviors are listed along with methods for improving these behaviors. You are sure to find your child's problem behaviors listed!

Main Points To Remember:

- This chapter gives you recommendations for common childhood problems such as ADHD, going to bed on time, resisting chores, bedwetting, daytime enuresis, and learning disorders.

- Effective methods for helping children improve their behavior include *encouragement, praise, racing the timer, sending a child to her room* (rather than time-out), *the resting chair, grounding*, and *point-rewards*.

- Contact a pediatrician, psychologist, or family counselor for more help if the child management methods that you're using aren't effective in helping your child.

Section Four

MORE RESOURCES FOR HELPING YOUR CHILD

You're not alone in the challenges of being a parent and assisting your son or daughter. Read this section and learn about various resources for parents.

Teachers spend many hours each week helping children. You'll learn how to work more effectively with your child's teacher to improve your child's academic and emotional adjustment.

Parent education classes are described and additional parenting books are recommended. You will learn when and how to get professional help for your child or family. A brief chapter tells how to control your own anger when you are confronted with the inevitable stresses of parenting.

The last chapter presents you with four brief quizzes and answers so you can test out what you have learned by studying SOS.

Let's look at resources for parents!

Chapter 20

Teachers And Parents As Partners

No one said that handling children is *easy*.

In this chapter, you'll learn how to help improve your child's classroom work and personal adjustment by working effectively with his teacher. You'll also learn about methods which teachers use to manage children.

Working With Your Child's Teacher

Build a positive relationship with your child's teacher and demonstrate an interest in your child's school experiences by visiting the classroom. Quickly respond to notes from the teacher and school. Even if you are working outside the home, volunteer to bring snacks or drinks for a class party. Your child will appreciate the additional attention and interest in her classroom.

If you have time, consider volunteering to help the teacher. After first discussing it with your son or daughter, donate some of your time to your child's class. You might arrange bulletin boards, organize bookshelves, or complete records.

Talk to your child about school. Discuss homework and special projects with your child, and spend some time looking at his completed assignments. The best way for you to increase his good work is to reward it with attention and praise. Post your child's school papers on the refrigerator door for the whole family to admire!

Don't say negative things about the teacher in your child's presence. You want your child to respect the teacher. Also, remember that children frequently repeat things to their teacher that they hear at home!

Parents should not defeat natural consequences by blaming the teacher or school for their child's behavior problems, or by conveying to their child that the school is wrong. Many parents feel personally attacked or inconvenienced when their child is disciplined by teachers. Receiving a mild correction can be a valuable learning experience for your child. Do cooperate with the school when your child is disciplined.

Sassy Janet *Doesn't* Stay After School

Nine-year-old Janet again had to stay after school for sassing her teacher. Janet's sassy talk was a continuing problem both at school and at home. Janet's mother usually gave Janet a ride home each afternoon after school and became annoyed with the teacher for making Janet stay after school. Janet's mother told the teacher, *"I don't like you keeping Janet after school for discipline. That punishes both Janet and myself. Find another method of discipline."* Janet's mother was herself a teacher at the local high school!

Plan ahead if you want a productive parent-teacher conference. *A parent-teacher conference is a face-to-face meeting between you and your child's teacher.* As partners, you plan the best way to meet your child's educational and personal needs. What do you talk about at a conference? You might discuss your child's study habits, need for remedial work, or how to help her get along better with other children.

The school will probably contact you and schedule at least one or two conferences a year. However, you have the right to ask for additional conferences if your child needs special help. Don't be passive and wait for the teacher to contact you if your child is having difficulties. Don't assume if you hear nothing from the teacher that everything is fine, especially if your child has had school problems in the past.

Consider the following guidelines when contacting your child's teacher for a conference.

1. Ask the teacher, at least a day in advance, to schedule a time to discuss your child's progress and adjustment. Don't just "drop in" on the teacher and expect to have a productive conference. To talk to the teacher about a problem or to schedule a conference, call the school and ask that the teacher return your call.

2. Make a list of things that you want to tell the teacher about your child, and make a list of questions that you have about your child's progress. Ask about your child's strongest and weakest subject areas and about any adjustment or behavior problems. If your spouse can't attend the conference, ask him or her for ideas when preparing your list.

3. Don't bring your child to the conference unless the teacher specifically requests that you bring her. Also, leave her brothers and sisters at home so that you and the teacher can devote full attention to discussing your child.

4. During the conference, decide on specific plans to help your child. Ask the teacher for suggestions and recommendations and honestly give these ideas a try. Agree on what the teacher is to do at school and what you are to do at home to help your child. Take notes concerning these future plans. Encourage the teacher to contact you if your child begins having problems at school.

5. Be pleasant and nurture a positive working partnership between you and the teacher. Tell the teacher that you appreciate the help that he or she is giving your child. If you feel that the teacher is doing a good job, let the teacher know it. Reward the teacher's "good behavior!"

Avoid getting upset and angry at the teacher and the school. Look for solutions to your child's problems, but avoid making the teacher feel responsible for those problems. Recognize that the teacher has at least 20 other children in the classroom. Understand the goals that the teacher and the school have for all children.

6. Following your meeting with the teacher, share the results of the conference with your spouse and ask for help in following through with any suggestions and

recommendations. After the conference, tell your child about his strengths, areas needing improvement, and any plan of action decided upon by you and the teacher.

    7. Keep in close touch with your child's teacher. Don't be afraid to ask for additional conferences. Teachers enjoy working with concerned parents who are strongly interested in their children. Teachers shouldn't mind additional conferences as long as you aren't blaming them for your child's problems.

    If your child's teacher agrees, use a *parent-teacher-child record form* to improve your child's school work or behavior problems. Each day, the child takes the record form between home and school. The teacher indicates on the form whether or not a particular undesired target behavior has occurred at school. When the child takes the record home, the parent can see if the target behavior occurred that day. The child then gains or loses a privilege at home that same afternoon or evening.

    For example, seven-year-old John completed his morning work only 62 percent of the time during a two-week period. He had the ability to do better, but he spent his time daydreaming and bothering children sitting near him. John's teacher asked John and his parents to attend a joint conference where it was agreed to use the record form to help him.

    Each day that John completed all of his morning work, he earned the privilege of watching television at home between 3:00 p.m. and 5:00 p.m. that afternoon. If he failed to complete his work or if he forgot the record form, then he couldn't watch television during those hours. John improved and instead of completing his work only 62 percent of the time, he completed it 94 percent of the time! See the *Parent-Teacher-Child Record Form* used to help John.

    Some record forms state that a privilege will be lost if a particular undesired target behavior such as fighting or teasing other children occurs. A record form provides your child, your child's teacher, and you with daily feedback regarding the child's progress with the target behavior. The record keeps everyone involved and coordinated in trying to improve the problem behavior. Since the record form requires extra time from the teacher, tell her that you appreciate her additional help.

    When your child is upset with other children, the teacher, or classwork, use *reflective listening* to help him to express his feelings and thoughts. Reflective listening skills are discussed in Chapter 18.

Parent-Teacher-Child Record Form —
Record Of John's Target Behavior

Record of ___*John's*___ Target Behavior
(child's name)

Week of: ___*January 7th to 11th*___

	M	T	W	T	F
Target behavior: _All morning work completed; yes or no_ (Teacher records each day)	No	No	Yes	Yes	Yes
Teacher's initials: (Teacher signs each day)	CC	CC	CC	CC	CC
Child's initials: (Child signs each day)	ib	ib	ib	ib	ib
Parent's initials: (parent signs each evening)	MB	MB	MB	MB	MB

Plan: _If John completes all morning work, he gets to watch television at home between 3:00 p.m. and 5:00 p.m. If work is not completed, or if John fails to bring this form home, then no television between 3:00 p.m. and 5:00 p.m._

Each day that John completes his work at school, he gets the privilege of watching television at home that afternoon. For a copy of a *Parent-Teacher-Child Record Form* see the tear-out sheets at the end of this book.

If your child continues to have difficulty with her schoolwork, you might consider obtaining a psychological evaluation of her educational skills, intellectual abilities, and level of motivation. The school might provide this evaluation. If not, you'll need to contact a psychologist yourself. Chapter 22 tells when and how to get professional help.

Teachers Managing Behavior

Read this section if you are interested in methods teachers may use in managing children.

PROBLEMS TEACHERS FACE

"My little Scott is a BITER. He bites EVERYONE. I hope that you can do something with him!"

Teachers must deal with a wide range of behavior problems.

Teachers state that the most difficult and stressful part of their job is managing behavior. Effective classroom teachers skillfully use a wide variety of behavior management methods. Other teachers are less effective, use a narrower range of methods, and misuse some methods.

Effective teachers know that rewarding good behavior is the best way to improve behavior. They frequently use *activity and material rewards* as well as *social rewards* such as praise and attention.

The Video SOS Help For Parents program and the SOS book also are used in teacher training programs and for in-service teacher training. See behavior management video clips at www.sosprograms.com

"Three Cheers For The Token Jar!"

Mrs. Clark wanted an effective way to help her second graders improve their problem behavior. Alicia was often out of her seat, roaming about the classroom. Robert couldn't see the chalkboard or his work unless he wore his glasses. However, he usually left them at home. Adam couldn't keep his hands to himself, and he often pushed and hit others. Lori rarely completed her work and spent most of her time daydreaming or trying to talk to other children.

One morning Mrs. Clark brought some poker chips and a clear plastic jar to school. The jar had a black line on it. Holding the jar and poker chips up for her class to see, she announced, *"Each of you may earn tokens and put them in the token jar. You can earn tokens by behaving in ways that help you or help our class. When the tokens come up to this black line, all of you will get a treat!"*

Alicia earned tokens by staying in her seat. Robert got a token for the jar when he remembered to wear his glasses to school. The teacher gave Adam a token when he went one hour without hitting or pushing anyone. The teacher *"caught" other children being good* and rewarded them with tokens too. When earning a token, the children also received approving smiles from their classmates.

The students were excited Friday afternoon because the tokens were almost touching the black line. All the students cheered when Alicia earned two tokens for turning in her work. When she dropped her tokens in the jar, the accumulated tokens came up to the black line. Mrs. Clark then gave each child a small candy bar. She also announced that the class could earn another reward — extra recess time for everyone — by filling the jar again.

Since all the children may earn tokens and all share in the eventual reward, the children give each other a lot of encouragement for demonstrating positive behavior. A *token jar* is an effective way to increase a variety of desirable behaviors without any record keeping.

Teachers also use *scolding and disapproval* as well as *active ignoring* to reduce problem behavior. *Behavior penalty, natural consequences,* and *logical consequences,* described in Chapter 5, are other effective discipline methods.

Trading A Dry Shirt For A Wet One

Shane splashed water in the school rest room and drenched Joshua's shirt! Shane also laughed and poked fun at Joshua and his wet shirt.

When both boys returned to their fourth grade classroom, the teacher made them trade shirts. Shane got to "wear" the problem he caused — the wet shirt! To deal with the problem behavior, the teacher used a *logical consequence* — Shane's correction fit his crime!

Many preschool and elementary teachers use *time-out* for handling persistent problem behavior.* Your child may refer to the "quiet chair," the "lonesome chair," or simply the "chair" when telling you about time-out. If your child tells you about being placed in time-out, listen, and avoid scolding her or expressing annoyance at her teacher. You want your child to tell you about all of her school experiences.

"Todd Put Patti In Time-Out Today!"

Although only two and a half years old, my son Todd was "experienced" in the time-out method. My wife and I used time-out to manage his misbehavior at home, and his day-care center also employed time-out.

Late one afternoon when my wife picked up Todd, she asked one of the day-care workers how Todd's day had gone. The worker responded, *"Guess what happened! Todd put Patti in time-out today!"* She further explained, *"I came into the playroom and found Patti, who is also two, quietly sitting on the time-out chair with Todd standing nearby. I asked what happened. Todd said that he made Patti get on the chair because she was 'bad' and threw blocks!"*

At the young age of two, Todd had already become an "old hand" with the time-out method.

Some teachers suspend a timer from the ceiling, out of the reach of active children. Since two children often misbehave at the same time, two separate time-out places and two timers are needed in a classroom.

---

*If you are a teacher and want a brief description of time-out to post or give to parents, reproduce a copy of the sheet "Information For Parents," included at the end of this book.

Bart Attacks The Preschool Timer

Four year old Bart, appeared to be patiently sitting on the time-out chair waiting for the timer to finally ring. When it rang, he slowly got down from the chair, walked to where the timer was setting on the floor, and then proceeded to stomp and kick it to pieces!

His teacher purchased a new timer, tied it to a string, and suspended it from the ceiling, well out of the reach of Bart and other preschoolers who disliked timers.

Three versions of time-out may be used to help improve the behavior of school children.

"NON-EXCLUSION" TIME-OUT

"All I did was HIT Jonathan once!"

1. Non-exclusion time-out. The child isn't excluded from the group. She is seated alone at a particular place or on a special chair. She can still observe group activities, but she can't participate. Other children are told not to tease or talk to a child who is in time-out. If they do, then they run the risk of being sent to time-out also!

2. Isolation time-out. If your child is in isolation time-out, he is briefly isolated from the group and all activities. He can't see or talk to the others. A good place for isolation time-out is on a large chair placed behind a file cabinet, screen, or bookcase. Isolation time-out frequently is more effective than non-exclusion time-out in changing behavior.

"ISOLATION" TIME-OUT

"I wish I had a book to look at or something to play with!"

3. Separate room time-out. The child is removed from other children and interesting activities and is briefly placed in a separate room. She isn't required to sit any particular place and is free to move around the room. The room should be boring, well-lighted, safe, and not scary. Separate room time-out shouldn't be used with preschoolers since, for safety's sake, they should always be monitored by adults.

Main Points To Remember:

- Keep in close touch with the teacher to improve your child's behavior at school.

- Demonstrate an interest in your child's school experiences by visiting the classroom and by talking to him about school.

- Effective classroom teachers, as well as effective parents, skillfully use a wide variety of SOS behavior management methods. Teachers also need to avoid making the nine common time-out mistakes.

Chapter 21

Helpful Classes And Books For Parents

"Wow! I'm going to try this idea!"

You'll want to continue learning additional parenting skills. This chapter tells how to join a parent education class or organize a parent study group. We'll also look at additional books which teach more parenting skills.

Joining Parent Education Classes — What To Expect

Parent education classes are offered in most communities. The classes will provide you with increased knowledge and skills in helping your child. Usually six to twelve parents and a group leader meet for five to ten sessions, with each session lasting one or two hours.

Leaders of parent education classes teach by using CDs, audiotapes, or videos and by directing the group discussion. The group members learn principles of behavior and parenting strategies which are important in assisting all children, not just children with emotional or behavioral problems. These classes are not therapy sessions, and the group leader won't attempt to diagnose or treat the problems of individual children.

Some parents who participate in parent education classes may have children who are experiencing significant emotional or behavioral problems. However, parent education classes usually deal with the normal challenges of child rearing faced by most parents.

Class leaders may follow the behavioral approach or they may use another approach. You'll find that behavioral parent education classes are particularly consistent with SOS.

How do you find out about parent education classes in your community? These classes may be offered at child guidance clinics, adult education centers, mental health centers, schools, churches, synagogues, community centers, and child development and psychology departments of universities. You may need to call several of these organizations in order to learn about the current classes scheduled in your community. Local crisis telephone lines also provide non-crisis information and may know about parenting classes in your area.

Forming An SOS Study Group

Consider forming a small informal study group with other parents and discussing common problems of rearing children. Your discussions could center around a particular topic or child management book such as *SOS Help For Parents.* Parents whose children are about the same age form a group. They have weekly meetings at each other's homes, at church, or at some other place in the community. Toddlers can play while parents talk. However, normally it's more relaxing for parents to meet while their children are at preschool or elementary school.

To begin a parent study group, all you need are three or four parents who are interested in meeting together. You might consider organizing such a group yourself. In order for meetings to continue, a group member should agree to act as a coordinator or discussion leader for each succeeding meeting. Avoid letting one parent dominate the group discussion. Don't discuss a son or daughter in front of that child or in the presence of other children.

SOS Programs & Parents Press offers enjoyable study materials for parenting classes and study groups.

The Video SOS Help For Parents is intended for parent groups and is to be shown in three or more sessions. Parenting scenes demonstrating SOS principles are shown, and a group leader guides the discussion following each of the scenes. Minimal preparation is needed for the leader. The easy-to-use Video Leader's Guide offers discussion questions for each of the scenes and offers guidelines for presenting the program. The SOS book and time-out CD (or audiotape) are necessary for an SOS study group. However, the SOS Video is not necessary.

How To Use Time-Out Effectively, a 67 minute CD (or audiotape), demonstrates and teaches time-out skills. Time-out is demonstrated with Todd who is two years old at the time of the recording. Todd (at age nine) and Lisa (age eleven) tell how they feel about time-out. You'll hear answers to common time-out questions and learn to avoid common time-out mistakes. This program is intended for individual listening and for study groups.

The book, *SOS Help For Parents,* is a self-administering program for use by parents wanting to learn additional skills for helping children. Suppose that your group meets six times and will use only the SOS book and audiotape. The following plan works well. Your group could be self-directed or counselor led.

Planning A Six Session SOS Study Group

Session One: Discuss chapters 1 & 2.

Session Two: Discuss chapters 3 & 5.

Session Three: Discuss chapters 4 & 6 to 12.

Session Four: Listen to and discuss the first half of the time-out CD or audiotape.

Session Five: Listen to and discuss the second half of the time-out CD or audiotape. Discuss SOS chapters 15 & 16 on time-out.

Session Six: Discuss SOS chapters 13, 14, and the remaining chapters. Chapter 18, "Helping Your Child Express Feelings," could merit one discussion session by itself.

Other Helpful Books For Parents

Your local book store will be willing to order the following books. I wrote the next book which I intend for adult and adolescent readers.

Clark, L. (2002). *SOS Help For Emotions: Managing Anxiety, Anger, And Depression.* Bowling Green, KY: SOS Programs & Parents Press. Illustrated. Although not specifically a parenting book, *SOS Help For Emotions* teaches how to manage anxiety, anger, depression and other unpleasant emotions. It will help you to improve your emotional intelligence. See the end pages of this book for ordering information. You can read a couple of chapters at www.sosprograms

The Merck Manual Of Medical Information: Second Home Edition (2003) at <www.merck.com/pubs/mmanual> is my favorite book and website for information on adult and child health problems and treatments. The website is a valuable free resource, although somewhat technical. For information on a variety of medications go to www.drugdigest.org.

Parenting Young Children
Write SOS Programs & Parents Press and request current information and a catalog of *SOS Programs*. Also, visit the SOS website at www.sosprograms.com There are free video clips, audio clips, and printed guides which may be downloaded by parents, educators, and counselors.

Schaefer, C. (1994). *How to Talk to Your Kids About Really Important Things*. San Francisco, CA: Jossey-Bass Publishers.
This unique book gives parents the words to use when talking to children about more than 30 important, sensitive issues such as a new baby in the family, going to the doctor, repeating a grade, and pornography. Teachers will also find the author's suggestions useful.

Barrish, H. & Barrish, I. (1989). *Managing And Understanding Parental Anger*. Kansas City, MO: Westport Publishers.
The forward by psychologist, Albert Ellis, states that this is the best available book on managing parental anger.

Dinkmeyer, D. & McKay, G. (1989). *The Parent's Handbook: Systematic Training for Effective Parenting.* Circle Pines, MN: American Guidance Service.
This illustrated book has a humanistic-Adlerian orientation and presents the principles of Rudolf Dreikurs and Thomas Gordon.

Faber, A. & Mazlish, E. (1980). *How To Talk So Kids Will Listen & Listen So Kids Will Talk.* NY: Avon.
This illustrated book teaches effective communication skills to parents.

Faber, A. & Mazlish, E. (1987). *Siblings Without Rivalry.* NY: W. W. Norton.
This book tells how to reduce conflict between your children.

Patterson, G. (1975). *Families: Applications Of Social Learning to Family Life.* Champaign, IL: Research Press.
Basic principles of behavior are discussed.

Classic Parenting Books
These classic books have not been updated but they continue to be highly regarded.

Dreikurs, R. & Soltz, V. (1964). *Children: The Challenge.* NY: Hawthorne.
The orientation of this book is similar to the orientation of the books by Drs. Dinkmeyer and McKay.

Ginott, H. (1965). *Between Parent and Child.* NY: Avon.
The author tells parents how to communicate with children and how to build mutual respect between parent and child.

Gordon, T. (1970). P.E.T.: *Parent Effectiveness Training.* NY: Plume.
This approach to child-rearing stresses reflective listening and other communication skills for parents.

Parenting Attention Deficit Disorder Children
Goldstein, S. & Goldstein, M. (1992). *Hyperactivity Why Won't My Child Pay Attention.* NY: John Wiley & Sons.
This book is a good resource for parents of ADHD and ADD children.

Ingersoll, B. (1988). *Your Hyperactive Child*. NY: Doubleday.
This is a parents' guide for helping children with attention deficit disorder.

Ingersoll, B. & Goldstein, S. (1993). *Attention Deficit Disorder And Learning Disabilities*. NY: Doubleday.
This book for parents discusses attention deficit disorder and learning disabilities.

Single Parents, Stepfamilies, And Divorce

Einstein, E. & Albert, L. (1986). *Strengthening Your Stepfamily*. Circle Pines, MN: American Guidance Service.
The authors tell parents how to strengthen the couple relationship and their family.

Kalter, N. (1990). *Growing Up With Divorce*. NY: The Free Press.
This book is written for divorced parents and provides information for helping children avoid emotional problems.

Parenting Teenagers

Dinkmeyer, D. & McKay, G. (1990). *Parenting Teenagers: Systematic Training for Effective Parenting of Teens*. Circle Pines, MN: American Guidance Service.
This is one of the better books for parents of teenagers.

Patterson, G. & Forgatch, M. (1987). *Parents and Adolescents Living Together - Part 1: The Basics*. Champaign, IL: Research Press.
This first of two volumes presents effective behavioral methods that parents of teenagers can employ in order to improve family life.

Patterson, G. & Forgatch, M. (1989). *Parents and Adolescents Living Together - Part 2: Family Problem Solving*. Champaign, IL: Research Press.

Main Points To Remember:

- Consider taking a parent education class.

- Organize an SOS parent study group. Follow the plan on page 181.

- Go to www.sosprograms.com and view and listen to the free video and audio clips. Download the free SOS Time-Out Guidelines and SOS Child Management Guidelines. Read chapters from *SOS Help For Emotions* at the website.

Chapter 22

When And How To Get Professional Help

"Can family counseling help us with our little Tiffany?"

Raising your child from infancy through adolescence is a long and sometimes difficult journey. Problems can arise and interfere with your family's well-being and happiness. If difficulties persist in spite of your efforts to resolve them, avoid giving in to hopelessness, inactivity, guilt, depression, or anger. Contact a counselor or therapist for professional help. Consider the following questions and suggestions when thinking about counseling for your child or family.

Q: *"When should I get professional help for my child?"*

A: As a parent, it's your responsibility to help your child and family to understand and solve problems. *Consider getting professional help if your child is persistently unhappy or has significant difficulty in adjusting to*

B. F. Skinner gave me permission to use the above cartoon in SOS.

school, peers, or other family members. Professional help may also be needed if your child is causing you or other family members a lot of distress. You may feel that your usual methods of managing your child aren't working or that your child's behavior is beyond control. If your child becomes violent when disciplined or won't cooperate with the time-out method, then you and your child may need some direct help from a professional counselor.

Q: *"How do I learn about professional counseling services in my area?"*

A: It often requires a lot of effort to learn about competent counselors and appropriate helping agencies in your community. Most pediatricians and family physicians can advise you about local family therapists and counselors. Ask your physician to recommend the names of at least two counselors. Some physicians may prematurely reassure worried parents with, *"Your child is just going through a stage"* or, *"He'll outgrow all those problems."* Consider what your physician says, but also discuss the indications and benefits of counseling with one of the counselors.

When contacting your pediatrician or physician, you may wish to discuss the possibility of a complete physical examination for your child before counseling begins. If your pediatrician suggests medication to help control your child's behavior, you might consider getting a second opinion from another pediatrician. Several books listed in Chapter 21 discuss medication and behavior.

Other sources of information about counselors or appropriate agencies include school principals and counselors, teachers, ministers, and friends. Most telephone crisis lines and community mental health centers are also valuable sources of information about available counseling services. Telephone directories list psychiatrists, psychologists, marriage and family counselors, and clinical social workers.

If your child has a learning problem at school, he should be seen by a qualified psychologist for an evaluation that includes psychological testing. Most school systems provide a psychological evaluation with recommendations if a child is experiencing learning or behavior problems at school. However, the thoroughness of psychological evaluations provided by schools is quite variable. Also, schools don't provide parent-child counseling services.

Professionals who offer therapy and counseling to children and adults, include psychiatrists (M.D.), psychologists (Ph.D., Psy.D., M.A., or M.S.), marriage and family counselors (Ph.D., M.A., or M.S.), and clinical social workers (M.S.W.). Most states require that mental health professionals be certified or licensed.

Q: *"What do I ask the family counselor during our first contact?"*

A: After obtaining the names of a couple of counselors or counseling agencies, you will need to telephone a counselor or agency. If the counselor is in private-independent practice, make a list of questions, and ask to speak directly with the counselor. Briefly, tell the counselor the nature of your child's difficulties. Ask if he helps children with such difficulties. If not, ask whom he would recommend to help you and your child. Inquire about the training, experience, and certification he has for working with children and families. Ask about the cost of each visit, how many visits will probably be necessary, and over what period of time. When first beginning counseling, weekly visits are important.

You will be given an appointment to meet with an "intake worker" if you contact a *mental health agency* for professional services. After meeting with you and your child, the intake worker will discuss your child's difficulties with other professional staff members. The agency will decide which professional is available and qualified to help you and your child. Then the agency will set a second appointment for you to meet with your counselor.

Q: *"How do I tell my child that we are going to see a family counselor?"*

A: Use direct, simple language when telling your child that the family or the two of you are going to meet with a counselor. Be positive and tell your child that the counselor will help to solve problems. For example, you might say, *"Everyone in our family has been arguing a lot the last few months. We have an appointment with a counselor who will help us to understand our problems and to get along better."*

If your child has been receiving low grades in school, you might say, *"We're going to meet with a psychologist. She'll give you some tests, talk to you, and talk to me also. She'll offer us some ideas about how to help you with your schoolwork and grades. We have an appointment Wednesday afternoon."*

Four Approaches To Helping Children And Parents:

- *The counselor does therapy directly with the child.* Most parents probably expect this treatment method, although this approach by itself is limited in its effectiveness.

- *The counselor teaches parents new methods for helping and managing their child.* You also may be asked to participate in parent education classes or read parenting materials, perhaps SOS.

- *The counselor helps parents to understand and resolve their personal problems.* Such problems often include depression, life crises, or marital difficulties.

- *The counselor meets with the entire family in counseling sessions.* Some problems are best treated by working with the whole family at one time.

Q: "What should I expect when we begin counseling?"

A: The first couple of sessions will focus on evaluation and assessment. The counselor will help evaluate and clarify the problems confronting you and your family. Since your spouse is a central part of the family, he or she should also become involved in counseling. In addition to talking with you about your child's difficulties, the counselor will ask about the expectations and goals that you have as a parent. You'll fill out brief questionnaires and keep records of your child's behavior. The counselor will talk with your child and observe you and your child together.

Be willing to modify your expectations for counseling and be flexible in working with your counselor. However, always ask your counselor any questions that you may have. With your permission, the counselor may contact your child's teacher and recommend additional ways the school can help your child.

After evaluating the problems troubling you and your child, the counselor will help you to solve these difficulties. Depending upon the problems to be resolved, counselors may use one or more possible approaches.

Q: *"How do I pay for professional services?"*

A: Counseling costs money, but so do health care, education, transportation, family entertainment, going out to eat, and vacations. Counseling can help to reduce your child's behavioral and emotional problems and to increase his personal competence and social skills. It can improve the quality of family life.

Counselors in private-independent practice usually have a set fee for each counseling session. Community mental health agencies, however, usually charge on a sliding scale based on family income. To determine if your medical insurance might cover all or part of your expenses, check with your insurance company and talk with the counselor. If a public school system is providing psychological testing and evaluation, there won't be a charge. Your taxes pay for these services!

Main Points To Remember:

- Family and behavior problems sometimes become difficult for parents to handle.

- Counselors can help you and your family to resolve problems.

- Consider getting professional help if your usual methods of managing your child or handling family problems aren't working.

SOS Help For Emotions teaches how to manage anxiety, anger, and depression by changing self-talk and irrational beliefs. Read a chapter on anger at www.sosprograms.com

Cognitive behavior therapy rests on behavior therapy. They share principles of behavior change and are compatible with each other.

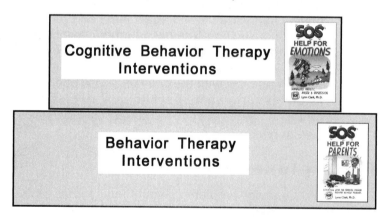

Cognitive Behavior Therapy Interventions

Behavior Therapy Interventions

SOS Help For Parents is a primer on behavior therapy for professionals and a handbook for helping children two to twelve.

SOS Help For Emotions: Managing Anxiety, Anger, & Depression is a primer for professionals on cognitive behavior therapy and is a self-help book for ages 12 to 90. It is not a parenting book. See the description on pages 243 to 246.

Chapter 23

Controlling Your Own Anger

MOTHER CONTROLS HER ANGER

"Please put away your toys and let's leave for school. We are late."

"NO! I'm gonna play some more!"

You can control your anger and your behavior when your child misbehaves and defies you.

Mother Controls Her Anger

Four-year-old Benjamin is often defiant and hard to handle. Mother has been working on improving her skills for managing Benjamin. More importantly, she has been using the STOP–THINK–ACT method for controlling her own anger. And she has stopped giving sarcasm, threats, and spankings to Benjamin.

Mother wants Benjamin to get ready to leave for school. Let's listen as she practices STOP–THINK–ACT to correct her old, irrational self-talk and aggressive discipline methods for trying to manage Benjamin.

191

Mother: *"Please put away your toys and let's leave for school. We are late."*

Benjamin: "No! I'm gonna play some more!"

(STOP) Mother realizes that Benjamin is not likely to mind her and that she is becoming hurtfully angry about this situation. She leaves the room and looks out a window for a minute.

(THINK) Mother says to herself, "I am making myself angry about this situation. What is my self-talk? What am I telling myself about Benjamin's defiant behavior to make myself angry? I think I am saying, Benjamin must experience pain if he is to learn who is boss. And if he doesn't learn to behave right now, he will always be a brat, and when he becomes an adult he will be an adult brat! But I don't have to make myself angry to improve his behavior. We will leave the house now and Benjamin will pick up his toys this afternoon, or he will get a time-out."

(ACT) Mother gets Benjamin's coat and shoes and returns to the room. They begin leaving for school.

Mother: *"Benjamin, we are leaving now. I have your coat and shoes and we are going to the car."*

Mother takes Benjamin by the arm and they walk out the door.

Benjamin: *"No! I don't want to go to Kiddie Kare. I don't have my shoes on. The last time I didn't have my shoes on, the kids made fun of me."*

Note - Benjamin feeling embarrassed about not having his shoes on when entering day care is a natural consequence for not getting ready on time.

Mother: "The helpers at Kiddie Kare will help you get your shoes on. Tomorrow we can get ready earlier." Mother and son walk out the door.

Good for mother! She is realizing that STOP–THINK–ACT and rational self-talk are helping her to control her anger and are helping Benjamin to improve his behavior.

Mother is also helping Benjamin to improve his behavior by setting a good example for him. Children learn how to control their anger by observing their parents. When children see parents lose control, children learn it's acceptable to lose control "when you get upset enough."

STOP – THINK – ACT Method

_____ Steps To Follow When You Begin To Feel Angry

STOP
Learn to recognize when you begin to feel angry.
Leave the situation.
Distract yourself with some 60 second activity.

THINK
Say to yourself, *"I am making myself angry about this situation."* Then ask yourself, *"What am I saying to myself about my child's misbehavior to make me hurtfully angry?"* Then say, *"I don't have to get angry to handle this behavior problem."* Your anger will likely decrease.

Decide which SOS method to use in handling the behavior problem.

Picture yourself using this SOS method to handle your child's misbehavior without expressing a lot of anger.

ACT
Briefly return to your child and the situation and implement the SOS method or plan you decided upon.

When you implement this SOS method, don't expect perfection of yourself or of your child.
Say to yourself, *"My child is not perfect, and I am not perfect. But I am working on controlling my anger and improving my parenting skills."*

When my daughter misbehaves she doesn't directly cause my anger. I cause my own anger by the way I view her misbehavior and by irrational self-talk statements about her behavior. I make myself intensely upset by whining that my child's behavior is horrible, awful, and that I can't stand it. Recognize that you can change your child's behavior without upsetting yourself.

As parents we control our anger by taking responsibility for our feelings of anger, as well as for our behavior when angry. We do this by acknowledging that our self-talk statements, and our beliefs and expectations for our child's behavior, directly control our feelings and behavior.

It's rational and helpful to feel only disappointed, annoyed, and irritated at our child. It's irrational to feel angry to such a degree that we might emotionally or physically hurt a child we love. Don't nurture and intensify hurtful anger.

Common Irrational Self-Talk Statements

"She won't think I am serious about her misbehavior unless I show how upset and angry I am."

"He should behave, he must behave, or I'm an awful, inadequate mother, and everybody will know it."

"Her misbehavior means she doesn't respect or care about me."

"His misbehavior will get worse and worse and he might eventually stop minding at all."

"She might grow up to be a delinquent, to be an irresponsible mother, etc."

"It's horrible and awful when he misbehaves. And I can't stand it."

"I have to let my anger and pent up emotions out, or I'll explode."

If you believe some of these statements, you will greatly intensify your anger. And you will be more likely to act in hurtful ways to your child and to yourself.

We can also manage our anger by knowing a variety of methods for dealing with our child's misbehavior. SOS teaches over 20 methods for handling more than 40 behavior problems.

Main Points To Remember:
• Realize that your child and unpleasant situations do not directly cause you to be angry.
• You cause your own anger by the way you view situations and by your self-talk statements.
• Use STOP–THINK–ACT and rational self-talk statements to control your anger.

My book, *SOS Help For Emotions: Managing Anxiety, Anger, And Depression* teaches methods for changing your thoughts and feelings. It is described in Chapter 21 and in the end pages of this book. Read chapters from *SOS Help For Emotions* at www.sosprograms.com

Chapter 24

Quizzes And Answers
For Parents

Each quiz asks 10 questions over a different section of SOS. Test your knowledge of the methods and skills described in SOS by marking the correct answers. Then check your answers with those given at the end of each quiz.

Quiz One
Chapter 1.   "Why Kids Behave And Misbehave"
Chapter 2.   "Clear Communication Promotes Effective Parenting"

Quiz Two
Chapter 3.   "Ways Of Increasing Good Behavior"
Chapter 5.   "Major Methods For Stopping Bad Behavior"

Quiz Three
Chapter 4.   "What is Time-Out? When Do Parents Use It?
Chapters 6 through 12.
            "Basic Skills Of The Time-Out Method"

Quiz Four
Chapters 13 through 18.
            "Further Applications Of Your Parenting Skills"

Note to educators and counselors: Four quizzes similar to these quizzes are available in the *DVD SOS Help For Parents* program and Kit.

Teach 19 basic child management skills to individuals or groups and measure how much parents learn using the Child Management Skills Test (CMST). The four quizzes and the Child Management Skills Test are reproducible and are included in the *DVD SOS Help For Parents* Kit. See the Order Form.

Quizzes And Answers For Parents

QUIZ ONE
Covering:
Chapter 1. "Why Kids Behave And Misbehave"
Chapter 2. "Clear Communication Promotes Effective Parenting"

Select the best answer to each question.

1.   When you reward any behavior, that behavior will:
       a. occur more often in the future.
       b. occur less often in the future.
       c. not change at all.
       d. stop occurring immediately.

2.   When praising a child, it's best to:
       a. give the child money along with praise.
       b. not praise too often.
       c. praise the specific behavior.
       d. all of the above are correct.

3.   An error or mistake commonly made by parents is:
       a. rewarding good behavior.
       b. correcting some bad behavior.
       c. rewarding good behavior quickly.
       d. failing to reward good behavior.

4.   Mike's tantrum in the grocery store earned him a candy
       bar. Mike's mother committed which error?
       a. failed to reward good behavior.
       b. accidentally correct good behavior.
       c. accidentally rewarded bad behavior.
       d. all of the above are correct.

5.   Parents should manage their child by:
       a. rewarding good behavior.
       b. not accidentally rewarding bad behavior
       c. using mild correction for some bad behavior.
       d. all of the above.

6.   A parent gives a command when:
a. the parent wants the child to stop or start a behavior but believes that a request will be disobeyed.
b. a simple request will be obeyed.
c. anytime a parent wants a child to stop a behavior.
d. anytime a parent wants a child to start a behavior.

7.   Clear communication between parents and between parent and child leads to:
a. agreement on "house rules."
b. fewer discipline problems.
c. better parenting.
d. all of the above are correct.

8.   A "house rule" that has been set up by *both parents and children:*
a. is *more* likely to be followed by the child.
b. is *less* likely to be followed by the child.
c. shouldn't be enforced by the parents.
d. leads to ineffective parenting.

9.   *"Put the cookie back!"* is an example of:
a. saying the child's name.
b. keeping the command simple.
c. backing up the command.
d. a stern facial expression.

10.   *"Look at him! He's always into something! I must be a bad, terrible parent."* This was probably said by:
a. an angry parent.
b. a hopeless parent.
c. a guilty parent.
d. a low energy parent.

Answers
1. a
2. c
3. d
4. c
5. d
6. a
7. d
8. a
9. b
10. c

Quizzes And Answers For Parents

QUIZ TWO
Covering:
Chapter 3. "Ways Of Increasing Good Behavior"
Chapter 5. "Major Methods For Stopping Bad Behavior"

Select the best answer to each question.

1.   Bill's parents actively ignore his sarcasm. They also
        praise him when he speaks politely. Bill's parents are:
        a. rewarding teasing.
        b. modeling bad behavior.
        c. rewarding good alternative behavior.
        d. all of the above are correct.

2.   Grandma's Rule simply says:
        a. never correct a child.
        b. the pleasant activity comes *after* the chore.
        c. the pleasant activity comes *before* the chore.
        d. give grandchildren lots of cookies!

3.   Diana's dad taught Diana how to play with the new puppy
        without hurting the animal. Diana's father was:
        a. correcting Diana for mistreating the puppy.
        b. helping Diana practice good behavior.
        c. using Grandma's Rule.
        d. using active ignoring.

4.   We increase our child's good behavior by:
        a. rewarding those behaviors.
        b. using active ignoring for some misbehavior.
        c. helping the child to practice good behavior.
        d. all of the above.

5.   Actively ignoring a whining child:
        a. will reward the whining behavior.
        b. will not change the child's behavior.
        c. will reduce the whining behavior in the long run.
        d. is impossible to do.

6. Any mild correction will be more effective if:
   a. parents only threaten to use it.
   b. no reason is given for the correction.
   c. parents remember to also praise the good alternative behavior.
   d. all of the above are correct.

7. Scolding is *not* an effective mild correction if your child:
   a. talks back to you when being scolded.
   b. ignores you or smiles when being scolded.
   c. has a temper tantrum when being scolded.
   d. all of the above are correct answers.

8. When Mary broke her little sister's doll, her parents gave one of Mary's dolls to the little sister. This is an example of:
   a. logical consequence.
   b. natural consequence.
   c. time-out.
   d. all of the above.

9. Tom lost his TV privileges because he stayed out past his curfew. This is:
   a. logical consequence.
   b. natural consequence.
   c. behavior penalty.
   d. scolding and disapproval.

10. Bad behavior may continue because:
    a. the rewards for the bad behavior outweigh the correction.
    b. the parents model or demonstrate the bad behavior themselves.
    c. parents rarely follow through with the mild correction.
    d. all of the above.

Answers
1. c
2. b
3. b
4. d
5. c
6. c
7. d
8. a
9. c
10. d

Quizzes And Answers For Parents

QUIZ THREE
Covering:
Chapter 4. "What is Time-Out? When Do Parents Use It?"
Chapter 6 through 12. "Basic Skills Of The Time-Out Method"

Select the best answer to each question.

1.   After time-out is over, parents should ask their child:
        a. *"Do you still love Mommy and Daddy?"*
        b. *"Can you say you're sorry?"*
        c. *"Will you promise to be good?"*
        d. *"Why did you have to go to time-out?"*

2.   Time-out is an effective way to reduce misbehaviors for
        children aged:
        a. one to five years old.
        b. two to twelve years old.
        c. six to twelve years old.
        d. ten to sixteen years old.

3.   Time-out *isn't* very useful in reducing:
        a. behaviors not seen by the parents.
        b. mocking or sassing parents.
        c. toy grabbing.
        d. spitting at others.

4.   The best time for demonstrating and explaining time-out
        to your child is:
        a. while you or your child is angry.
        b. before you ever use time-out.
        c. while you are using time-out for the first time.
        d. all of the above.

5.   The place chosen for time-out should be:
        a. dull, boring, and safe.
        b. the child's bedroom.
        c. a frightening place.
        d. where the child's toys are.

6.   A timer is a necessary part of time-out because:
     a. timers can't "forget" the child.
     b. children take responsibility for correctly leaving time-out.
     c. ticking timers let others know that "time-out is in progress."
     d. all of the above are correct.

7.   *"David! I can't believe that you're teasing your sister again! Go to time-out — this time for 20 minutes!"*
     David's father just made which error?
     a. only threatening to use time-out?
     b. using a very long period of time-out.
     c. not selecting the right place for time-out.
     d. all of the above.

8.   If your child screams during time-out, you should:
     a. scold the child for being noisy.
     b. stop using time-out.
     c. ignore the noise or add one to three minutes to time-out if he's noisy when the timer rings.
     d. give the child a behavior penalty or spanking.

9.   When a child is annoyed with her parents after being in time-out, her parents should:
     a. apologize for using-time out.
     b. ignore her complaints and realize that she has a right to her feelings.
     c. put her back into time-out.
     d. offer her a candy bar or ice-cream!

10. During the first few weeks of using time-out, parents should expect their son to:
     a. completely stop misbehaving.
     b. go to time-out without any fussing or complaining.
     c. apologize for his misbehavior.
     d. "test" and challenge his parents' new method of discipline.

Answers
1. d
2. b
3. a
4. b
5. a
6. d
7. b
8. c
9. b
10. d

Quizzes And Answers For Parents

QUIZ FOUR
Covering:
Chapters 13 through 18. "Further Applications Of Your Parenting
                                Skills"

Select the best answer to each question.

1.   Tokens and point-rewards may be exchanged for:
        a. praise.
        b. freedom from time-out.
        c. special privileges or inexpensive toys.
        d. all of the above.

2.   The best and easiest way to improve behavior is to:
        a. reward good behavior.
        b. correct bad behavior.
        c. use time-out.
        d. worry and fret a lot!

3.   A parent-child contract should be written down and
        include:
        a. duties of the child only.
        b. everyone's duties and consequences if the contract
           isn't upheld.
        c. no possibility for changing the contract.
        d. only the parents' signature.

4.   Timing-out both children reduces fighting because:
        a. both children get the same mild correction.
        b. parents aren't rewarding children with attention by
           scolding them.
        c. parents don't have to decide which child is guilty and
           which is innocent.
        d. all of the above are correct.

5.   An aggressive child's threats to injure another child should:
        a. result in time-out.
        b. be ignored.
        c. lead to a spanking.
        d. be given a lot of attention.

6.	Reflective listening requires a parent to:
	a. give the child attention when he expresses feelings.
	b. restate the child's feelings and the situation that the child describes.
	c. give advice or suggestions only *after* the child has expressed his feelings.
	d. all of the above.

7.	Point-reward calendars are effective because:
	a. children earn points for misbehaving.
	b. children can buy rewards with points earned.
	c. parents don't have to give praise.
	d. all of the above are correct.

8.	Before using time-out in public or when visiting friends:
	a. the child should be accustomed to time-out at home.
	b. parents should tell the child how she is expected to behave in public.
	c. parents should be prepared to deal with interference from others.
	d. all of the above.

9.	When two children keep fighting over a toy, a parent should:
	a. scold them into taking turns.
	b. put either the children or the toy in time-out.
	c. give the toy to a charity.
	d. buy each child a new toy.

10.	Reflective listening requires the parent to:
	a. scold the child if the child voices irrational plans.
	b. offer suggestions only *before* the child has expressed his feelings.
	c. offer suggestions only *after* the child has expressed his feelings.
	d. all of the above are correct.

Answers
1. c
2. a
3. b
4. d
5. a
6. d
7. b
8. d
9. b
10. c

Appendices

Valuable resources for helping children are described in the following appendices.

Appendix A describes the various components of the DVD SOS parent education and parent counseling programs. It also summarizes the two dominant approaches in parent education and parent counseling and how SOS integrates these approaches.

Appendix B provides SOS reminder sheets for parents and teachers which summarize the basic child rearing rules and methods emphasized throughout this parenting handbook. Download, for free, a color version of these and additional sheets at www.sosprograms.com

DVD Video
SOS
Help For Parents

A Video-Discussion

Parent Education &

Counseling Program

See free video clips in English & Spanish at
www.sosprograms.com

Appendix A

SOS Video
And Professional Materials

SCENE FROM THE SOS VIDEO (English & Spanish)

"Thanks for tying your sister's shoe!"

SOS Help For Parents is a book and video-based parent education program which helps children, ages two to twelve, improve their behavior and emotional adjustment. It is internationally recommended and used by psychologists, pediatricians, child psychiatrists, teachers, and other professionals, as well as parents. SOS teaches over 20 methods for helping children and offers the most complete instructions available for using time-out.

The goal of SOS is to help parents to be better parents, by improving their behavior management skills. Professionals who educate parents, counsel parents, or render services to children and families will find the SOS book and video useful educational and counseling tools. With over 100 illustrations, the *SOS Help For Parents* book is both enjoyable to read and easy to understand.

> *"The multi-media approach [of the SOS Help For Parents Programs] makes the information accessible to parents and children at all levels of adjustment and functioning."*
> – Journal of Marital And Family Therapy

English SOS

SOS Help For Parents
13 International
Editions
and Languages

Portuguese, Dutch (The Netherlands), and Estonian are additional editions.

Spanish SOS

Turkish SOS

Japanese SOS

Chinese SOS
Beijing Normal Univ

Korean SOS

Chinese SOS
Taiwan

Hungarian SOS

Arabic SOS

Icelandic SOS

The DVD/Video SOS Help For Parents

The SOS DVD/Video program is used by counselors, clinics, child treatment programs, parent groups, educators, houses of worship, day-care centers, Head Start centers, and social service professionals. The program is intended for parenting workshops, staff development, in-service training, teacher training, classroom use, and one-to-one parent counseling.

The *DVD/Video Leader's Guide* gives guidelines for presenting the program. Part One of the video may be viewed individually or with a group. See sample pages at www.sosprograms.com

For Part Two of the video, a group leader needs to guide the discussion following each of the 43 parenting scenes. The *DVD/Video Leader's Guide* offers discussion questions for each scene. Discussion questions for two of the parenting scenes are presented on pages 248 and 249 at the back of this book. Each participant receives a reproducible Parent Handout sheet listing 19 parenting rules, common errors, and methods for managing behavior. Using this Parent Handout, participants are asked to identify which of these parenting rules and methods a scene demonstrates. This teaching method provides both the group leader and participants with immediate feedback on how much the participants are learning. Allow about four one hour sessions to present the complete DVD/video-based program.

> For sample pages from the *DVD/Video Leader's Guide* see pages 248 & 249

Following the presentation of the SOS DVD/Video program, many leaders teach additional time-out skills using the "How To Use Time-Out Effectively" CD (or audiotape). Allow about five one hour sessions to present both the DVD/SOS Video program and audio program. Participants should learn time-out skills <u>after</u> learning the basic child rearing principles and skills presented in the DVD/Video program.

Technical Talk: The approach of the SOS Parenting program includes principles of learning and reinforcement, social learning, reflective listening, and humanistic-Adlerian psychology applied to helping children. The program is practical, clear, easy to understand, and rests on data-based research studies of behavior change. This DVD/video-based program, however, is easy to present and does not require training in the principles of learning. A Spanish DVD/video program also is available.

   The SOS Video includes much humor and is popular with parents and with professionals who help parents. Over 10,000 SOS video programs have been ordered throughout the world. All SOS DVDs play internationally, region free.
   The following materials are included in *The Video SOS Help For Parents* educational package.

   • 72 minute video in both DVD & VHS (same content). The video (in English or Spanish) employs 57 live action scenes and 11 cartoon scenes.

   • *Video Leader's Guide* in English.

   • Reproducible parent handouts in English and Spanish.

   • Child Management Skills Test (CMST) in English.

   • *SOS Help For Parents* book in English. The *SOS Ayuda Para Padres* book is included with Spanish video program.

Visit our website and learn how you can use The SOS Video to help educate or counsel parents in basic methods of behavior management. See free video and audio clips in English and Spanish at **www.sosprograms.com**

SOS Help For Parents & **SOS Ayuda Para Padres** (Books)
   In addition to parents, these handbooks are suggested for:

   • Family therapists, social services professionals

   • Parenting programs presented at community centers, social service agencies, houses of worship, mental health and counseling centers, preschools

   • Elementary teachers, special education classes kindergartens, preschools, day-care centers

   • Special programs for handicapped and "high risk" children. Pediatricians, clinics, hospitals

   • Colleges — courses in family therapy, behavior therapy, child development, parenting, special education, practicum, field placements

"How To Use Time-Out Effectively"
Audio Program on both CD & Audiotape

A brief Time-Out Guide and illustrated Time-Out Chart are included with this 67 minute audio program which teaches time-out skills. Todd (age nine) and Lisa (age eleven) tell how they feel about time-out. Parents hear answers to common time-out questions and learn to avoid nine common time-out mistakes. It is suitable for individual listening or for parent workshops. For more information see pages 60 and 66.

SOS, Behavior Therapy, and Cognitive Behavior Therapy

Cognitive behavior therapy rests on behavior therapy. They share principles of behavior change and are compatible with each other.

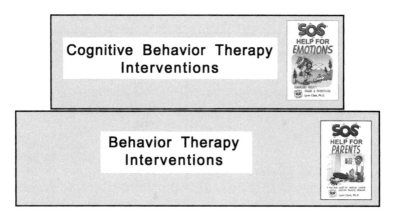

SOS Help For Parents is a primer on behavior therapy for professionals and a handbook for helping children two to twelve.

SOS Help For Emotions: Managing Anxiety, Anger, & Depression is a primer for professionals on cognitive behavior therapy and is a self-help book for ages 12 to 90. It is not a parenting book. See the description on pages 243 to 246.

Together, the two SOS books cover the age range from two through adulthood. Go to www.sosprograms.com and look for free *Resources for Counselors and Educators*.

Many professionals make SOS books available to clients when they most need them – *immediately!* Counselors also loan SOS books with a deposit. Clients can return books or keep them.

Child Management Skills Test (CMST)

The CMST assesses parents' knowledge of 19 Basic Child Management Rules, Errors, Methods, and Skills. Five easily scored objective tests over 43 parent-child scenes shown in The Video SOS Help For Parents comprise the CMST. The CMST Manual, Answer Sheets, and Scoring Keys may be downloaded at no charge from www.sosprograms.com

The illustration, "Theoretical Approaches In Parent Education," shows the history and development of the two dominant systems in parent education and parent counseling. The behavioral and the humanistic/Adlerian systems are the two major approaches to parenting. The illustration also shows the development of SOS.

Theoretical Approaches In Parent Education

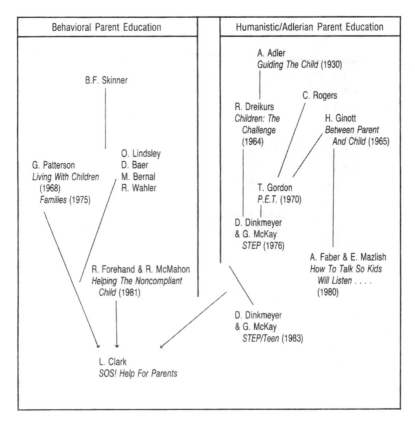

Both the behavioral and humanistic/Adlerian approaches present methods, materials, and training programs in parenting. The behavioral approach is producing impressive research data, documenting its effectiveness in improving behavior. The following table describes major differences between the two approaches.

Differences Between Behavioral And Humanistic/Adlerian

Parent Education

Differences	Behavioral	Humanistic/Adlerian
1. Method of research	Systematic observation, recording, and control of behavior; data-based	Case histories, anecdotes
2. Democratic emphasis in parenting	Less emphasis	More emphasis
3. Who can benefit?	Parents and children at all levels of adjustment and functioning	Parents and children at higher levels of adjustment and functioning
4. Communication of feelings between parent and child	Less emphasis	More emphasis

SOS Programs & Parents Press welcomes copies of data-based research studies involving SOS educational materials from researchers.

SOS Help For Parents book is available in English, Spanish, Korean, Chinese, Turkish, Hungarian, Icelandic, and Arabic. Publishers in other countries are requesting the rights to translate SOS into their languages as well.

Index

Index — 46 Problem Behaviors
And 23 SOS Methods

PROBLEM PARENTS FACE

"Do you want it? Hee, hee, hee!"

Does this remind you of your kids?

To use this index, look up a particular problem behavior which your child is demonstrating. Study various methods and strategies that you might use to help your child. The list, however, isn't intended to be used without first reading SOS, which describes the basic principles and methods for improving behavior.

After learning the basic SOS methods for improving behavior, you will find this Menu of Interventions for 46 problem behaviors to be useful for solving a variety of behavior problems. This Menu begins on page 233. Many counselors and other mental health professionals refer to this Index when developing intervention plans for helping specific children.

Appendix B

SOS Summary Sheets
For Parents

The following are reminder sheets for parents and teachers which summarize the main points described throughout *SOS Help For Parents*. They may be copied for personal use.

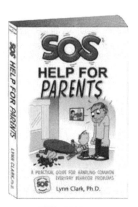

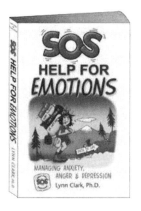

www.sosprograms.com

Basic Child Rearing Rules And Errors

What can you do to help your child improve his or her behavior? *Follow three basic child rearing rules and avoid four common errors.* These rules and errors are discussed in Chapter One of *SOS Help For Parents.*

Three Child Rearing Rules —

Parents' Check List

Rule #1. Reward good behavior (and do it quickly and often).*

Rule #2. Don't "accidentally" reward bad behavior.**

Rule #3. Correct some bad behavior (but use *mild* correction only).

"Accidentally" Causing Behavior Problems — Four Child Rearing *Errors To Avoid*

Error #1.   Parents fail to reward good behavior.

Error #2.   Parents "accidentally" correct good behavior.

Error #3.   Parents "accidentally" reward bad behavior.

Error #4.   Parents fail to correct bad behavior (when *mild* correction is indicated).

---

*When behavior is rewarded, that behavior receives "positive reinforcement" or simply "reinforcement."
**When behavior which once was rewarded is no longer rewarded, the term "extinction" is used. Extinction is also called nonreinforcement of behavior.

Rewards Children Like

"That's great! You're learning to tie your own shoes!"

It's important to reward your child's good behavior. Rewarding good behavior is the easiest and best way to improve behavior. What rewards should parents use? *Rewards that motivate children are social rewards, activity rewards, and material rewards.*

Rewards Children Like

Social Rewards	Activity Rewards Including Privileges	Material Rewards
Smiles	Play cards with mother	Ice cream
Hugs	Go to park	Ball
Pats	Look at book with father	Money
Attention	Help bake cookies	Book
Touching	Watch a late TV movie	Jump rope
Clap hands	Have a friend over	Balloons
Winks	Play ball with father	Yo-yo
Praise	Play a game together	Flashlight
"Good job"	Go out for pizza together	CD

It's also important to "fail to reward" your child's bad behavior. If you "accidentally" reward bad behavior, you will strengthen that bad behavior.

Reward only good behavior and do it quickly and often. Basic child rearing rules and common errors are discussed in Chapter 1 of *SOS Help For Parents.*

How To Give Effective Instructions And Commands To Your Child

All parents must be able to give clear, effective instructions and commands on occasion. They must also be able to "back up" their commands. A command is a request to immediately start or stop a behavior.

When are commands given? Give your child a command when you want him to *stop* a specific misbehavior *and* you believe that he might disobey a simple request to stop the misbehavior. Also, give a command when you want your child to *start* a particular behavior *and* you believe that your child might disobey a simple request to start the behavior:

How should you give a command? Follow the guidelines listed below:

Giving Effective Commands To Your Child

Parents' Check List

_____ Steps To Follow:

____ 1. Move close to your child.

____ 2. Have a stern facial expression.

____ 3. Say his or her name.

____ 4. Get and maintain eye contact.

____ 5. Use a firm tone of voice.

____ 6. Give a direct, simple, and clear command.

____ 7. "Back up" your command, if necessary.

Be sure to give "good" instructions and commands rather than "bad" instructions and commands. "Good" commands are clear, direct, and simple. "Bad" commands are unclear, indirect, vague, complicated, consist of chains of commands, or are given as questions.

What if your child doesn't obey your command? You have *time-out* — a useful back-up! The correct steps for using time-out and how to give effective commands are described in *SOS* .

Basic Steps For *Initially* Using Time-Out —

Parents' Check List

_____ **Steps To Follow:**	*A portable timer is essential for effective time-out!*

___ 1.   Select one target behavior on which to use time-out. (Chapter 4)

___* 2.   Count how often this target behavior occurs. (Chapter 4)

___ 3.   Pick out a boring place for time-out. (Chapter 7)

___ 4.   Explain time-out to your child. (Chapter 8)

___ 5.   Wait patiently for the target behavior to occur. (Chapter 9)

TARGET BEHAVIOR OCCURS!

___ 6.   Place your child in the time-out place and use no more than 10 words and 10 seconds. (Chapter 9)

___ 7.   Get the portable timer, set it to ring one minute for each year of age, and place it within hearing distance of your child. (Chapter 10)

___ 8.   Wait for the timer to ring — remove all attention from your child while she waits for the timer to ring. (Chapter 10)

___*9.   Ask your child, after the timer rings, why she was sent to time-out. (Chapter 11)

*These two steps are important but not essential.

Set the timer one minute for each year of your child's age. Always use a portable windup timer. The basic steps for using time-out are discussed in *SOS Help For Parents*. See a free video clip at www.sosprograms.com entitled "Time-Out, Effective Use." I describe time-out and time-out is demonstrated with five children.

Methods Of *Mild* Correction — Comparison For Parents

Method of Mild Correction	Age of Child	Effectiveness of Correction	Type of Behaviors Corrected	How Quickly Applied
Time-Out	Two through twelve	Extremely effective	Most behavior, especially hard-to-handle behavior	Immediately, if possible
Scolding and Disapproval	All Ages	Moderately effective	All Behavior	Immediately or later
Natural Consequences	All Ages	Effective	Some Behavior	Immediately or later
Logical Consequences *"I'm putting your crayons up for ONE WEEK!"*	Three through Adolescence	Effective	Most Behavior	Immediately or later
Behavior Penalty For example, *"No TV for rest of the day."* or *"No bike riding for rest of the day."*	Five through Adolescence	Effective	All Behavior	Immediately or later

Basic Steps For Handling Aggressive Or Dangerous Behavior — Parent's Check List

**Immediate Steps
____ To Follow:**

___ 1. Stop the behavior.

___ 2. Deliver a brief scolding and name the unacceptable behavior.

___ 3. Place him in time-out immediately.

After Time-Out Is Over:

___ 4. Ask him to say what he did that was aggressive or dangerous.

___ 5. Help him describe one or two other ways of behaving safely or nonaggressively in the future. Reward him with your praise after he tells you about these safer ways of behaving.

___ 6. Follow through with a mild logical consequence or behavior penalty. (See Chapter 5)

___ 7. Use reflective listening *if* your child is in the mood to talk. (Chapter 18)

Chapter 17 of *SOS Help For Parents* discusses the basic steps for handling aggressive or dangerous behavior.

Giving Feelings A Name

NAMES FOR PLEASANT FEELINGS

SOS

accepted, liked	glad
appreciated	good, great
capable, confident	grateful, thankful
successful	pleased
comfortable, relaxed	love, loved
eager	satisfied, happy
cheerful, elated	enjoy, like
hopeful, optimistic	proud
encouraged	respected
relieved	secure, safe

NAMES FOR UNPLEASANT FEELINGS

angry, mad	unhappy, miserable
resentful, want to get even	messed over, unfair
irritable, grumpy	unloved, neglected
scared, afraid	discouraged
disappointed, let down	embarrassed
lonely, left out	hurt
without a friend, rejected	tired
worthless, no good	bored
stupid, dumb	confused
upset, tense	frustrated
worried, anxious	inferior
insecure	guilty

These two lists give labels for common pleasant and unpleasant feelings experienced by both children and adults. For a convenient pocket card, photocopy this sheet, cut inside the lines, fold, and tape.

Help your child to name his or her feelings. Naming feelings is essential to understanding and managing them. Chapter 18 of *SOS Help For Parents* describes the basic steps for "Helping Your Child To Express Feelings."

Point-Reward Calendar

For Improving *One* Behavior

POINTS EARNED							
Good Behavior (and possible points):							
	S	**M**	**T**	**W**	**T**	**F**	**S**
First Week							
Second Week							
Third Week							

This calendar records one behavior for several weeks. At the end of the third week, post a new calendar.

When your child spends a point, draw a red mark or slash through that point. Points without slash marks are points not yet spent. Encourage your child to spend her points rather than save them because spending points is more reinforcing for your child.

Chapter 14 of *SOS Help For Parents* describes how to use a point-reward calender.

Point-Reward Calendar

For Improving *Several* Behaviors

POINTS EARNED							
List of Good Behavior (and possible points)	S	M	T	W	T	F	S
TOTAL POINTS EARNED							

This calendar provides a record of several kinds of behaviors for one week. Post a new calendar each week.

At the end of each day, total the number of points your child has earned. Draw marks through the points on the bottom line when your child spends those points.

Chapter 14 of *SOS Help For Parents* describes how to use a point-reward calender to improve behavior.

Menu Of Rewards

Menu Of Rewards	
<u>Reward</u>	<u>Cost in</u> <u>points</u>

List material rewards and activity rewards on this menu. Also list the number of points or tokens that your child must pay for each reward. Post this menu next to the point-reward calendar.

Chapter 14 of *SOS Help For Parents* describes how to use a menu of rewards to improve behavior.

Parent-Child Contract Form

CONTRACT

I,_____, agree to: _____
_{child's name}

_____

_____

Mother and Father, agree to: _____

_____

_____

_____

_____

_____

Date contract begins: _____

Date contract ends: _____

_____

Date contract signed: _____

Agreed to by: _____
(Child's Signature)

_____
(Mother)

_____
(Father)

How to use parent-child contracts is described in Chapter 14 of *SOS Help For Parents*.

Parent-Teacher-Child Record Form

Record of _____ Target Behavior
(child's name)

Description of target behavior to be increased or decreased:

_____

Week of: _____

	M	T	W T	F	
Target behavior: (Teacher records, yes or no, each day if the target behavior occurs.)					
Teacher's initials: (Teacher signs each day)					
Child's initials: (Child signs each day)					
Parent's initials: (parent signs each evening)					

Plan: _____

_____

_____

Chapter 20 of *SOS Help For Parents* describes how to use parent-teacher-child record forms to improve your child's school work or personal adjustment at school.

Information For Parents

"All I did was HIT Jonathan once!"

Dear Parents,

All classrooms have behavior problems from time to time. Time-out is a safe, nonaggressive way for helping children to improve their behavior. Time-out is placing a child in a dull, boring place for a brief period of time following the child's misbehavior.

Time-out is used for hitting, kicking, shoving, scratching, biting, spitting at others, behavior dangerous to oneself, and threatening others. Sometimes children are placed in time-out for grabbing things from others, repeatedly disobeying classroom rules, swearing, angry screeching, and sassy talk to me.

You shouldn't discipline your child at home if you find out that he was placed in time-out at school. You want your child to feel free to tell you about what is happening at school!

Time-out can also be used to help correct a child's misbehavior at home. Please ask me any questions that you may have about time-out or other methods that I use to help children.

_____

(teacher)

ANGER – USED AS AN INSTRUMENT
TO GET WHAT YOU WANT

"Get me a Coke! Get me a Coke NOW!"
(from the SOS DVD)

Instrumental anger is the anger a child uses as an instrument or lever, to pressure others to give him what he wants. Unfortunately, some parents give in and accidentally reward their child for using anger, a fit, or emotional upsetness as an instrument for controlling the family and others.

For example, only when Michael expresses increasing anger does mother give in and give him both ice cream and a Coke. Earlier, she had told him *"no dessert"* because he didn't eat his supper.

What is Michael believing and telling himself that causes him to behave aggressively? At a low level of self-awareness, Michael is saying to himself, *"Mother must give me that Coke and if she doesn't, it's awful and I-can't-stand-it! I must have that Coke! I'm going to get real upset, and then she'll give in!"*

Michael has accidentally learned to use emotional upsetness and anger to get what he wants. If this way of thinking and acting becomes a habit, he will be at high risk for experiencing emotional and behavioral problems as an adolescent and adult.

To see a brief video clip of this example (in either English or Spanish) along with solutions parents can implement, go to "Rewarding Bad Behavior" at **www.sosprograms.com**

REFERENCES

American Psychiatric Association. (1994). *Diagnostic and statistical manual of mental disorders.* (4 th. ed.). Washington, DC: Author.

Bandura, A., & Walters, R. H. (1963). *Social learning and personality development.* NY: Holt, Rinehart & Winston.

Barkley, R. A. (1981). *Hyperactive children: A handbook for diagnosis and treatment.* NY: Guilford Press.

Barrish, H., & Barrish, I. (1989). *Managing and understanding parental anger.* Kansas City, MO: Westport Publishers.

Bernal, M. E. (1984). Consumer issues in parent training. In R. F. Dangel & R. A. Polster (Eds.), *Parent Training: Foundations of research and practice.* (pp. 477-546). NY: Guilford Press.

Bernal, M. E., & North, J. A. (1978). A survey of parent training manuals. *Journal of Applied Behavior Analysis, 11,* 533-544.

Brooks, N., Perry, V., & Hingerty, E. (1992). Modifying behavior through time-out from positive reinforcement. *Vocational Evaluation and Work Adjustment Bulletin, 25,* 93-95.

Christophersen, E. R. (1990). *Beyond discipline.* Kansas City, MO: Westport Publishers.

Clark, L. (1972). *Time out and 10-10-10.* Unpublished manuscript.

Clark, L. (1989). *The time-out solution.* NY: Contemporary Books. This condensed version of *SOS Help for parents* was available from 1989 to 1994.

Clark, L. (1998). SOS help for emotions:Managing anxiety, anger, and depression. Bowling Green, KY: Parents Press.

Corey, G. (1996). *Theory and practice of counseling and psychotherapy.* (5th ed.). Pacific Grove, CA: Brooks/Cole Publishing Company.

Curran, D. (1989). *Working with parents.* Circle Pines, MN: American Guidance Service.

Dangel, R. F., & Polster, R. A. (1988). *Teaching child management skills.* NY: Pergamon Press.

DeRisi, W. J., & Butz, G. (1975). *Writing behavioral contracts: A Case simulation practice manual.* Champaign, IL: Research Press

Dinkmeyer, D., & McKay, G. (1989). *The parent's handbook: systematic training for effective parenting.* Circle Pines, MN: American Guidance Service.

Dinkmeyer, D., & McKay, G. (1990). *Parenting teenagers: systematic training for effective parenting of teens.* Circle Pines, MN: American Guidance Service.

Dreikurs, R., & Soltz, V. (1964). *Children: The challenge.* NY: Hawthorn Books.

Dryden, W., & DiGiuseppe, R. (1990). *A primer on rational-emotive therapy.* Champaign, IL: Research Press.

Egan, G. (1990). *The skilled helper: A systematic approach to effective helping.* (4th ed.). Pacific Grove, CA: Brooks/Cole Publishing Company.

Ellis, A. (1994). *Reason and emotion in psychotherapy.* NY: Birch Lane.

Fee, V., Matson, J., & Manikam, R. (1990). A control group outcome study of a nonexclusionary time-out package to improve social skills with preschoolers. *Exceptionality*, 1, 107-121.

Faber, A., & Mazlish, E. (1980). *How to talk so kids will listen & listen so kids will talk.* NY: Avon.

Forehand, R. (1993). Twenty years of research on parenting: Does it have practical implications for clinicians working with parents and children? *The Clinical Psychologist*, 46, 169-176.

Forehand, R. L., & McMahon, R. J. (1981). *Helping the noncompliant child.* NY: Guilford Press.

Fox, R., Fox, A., & Anderson, R. (1991). Measuring the effectiveness of the Star parenting program. *Psychological Reports*, 68, 35-40.

Gast, D. L., & Nelson, C. M. (1977). Legal and ethical considerations for the use of timeout in special education settings. *Journal of Special Education,* 11, 457-467.

Ginott, H. (1965). *Between parent and child.* NY: Avon.

Ginott, H. (1971). *Between parent and teenager.* NY: Avon.

Goldstein, S., & Goldstein, M. (1992). *Hyperactivity why won't my child pay attention.* NY: John Wiley & Sons.

Gordon, T. (1970). *P.E.T.: Parent effectiveness training.* NY: Plume.

Hansen, D. J., Tisdelle, D. A., & O'Dell, S. L. (1984). Teaching parents time-out with media materials: The importance of observation and feed-back. *Child and Adolescent Psychiatry, 1,* 20-25.

Harris, T. (1967). *I'm ok — You're ok.* NY: Avon.

Hobbs, S. A., & Forehand, R. (1977). Important parameters in the use of timeout with children: A re-examination. *Journal of Behavior Therapy and Experimental Psychiatry, 8,* 365-370.

Hobbs, S. A., Forehand, R., & Murray, R. G. (1978). Effects of various durations of timeout on the noncompliant behavior of children. *Behavior Therapy, 9,* 652-659.

Horn, A. M., & Sayger, T. V. (1990). *Treating conduct and oppositional defiant disorders in children.* NY: Pergamon Press.

Lindsley, O. R. (1966). An experiment with parents handling behavior at home. *Johnstone Bulletin, 9,* 27-36.

Long, P., Forehand, R., Wierson, M., Morgan, A. (1994). Does parent training with young noncompliant children have long-term effects? *Behavior Research and Therapy, 32,* 101-107.

Ingersoll, B. (1988). *Your hyperactive child.* NY: Doubleday.

Ingersoll, B., & Goldstein, S. (1993). *Attention deficit disorder and learning disabilities.* NY: Doubleday.

Martin, G., & Pear, J. (1996). *Behavior modification: What it is and how to do it.* (5th ed.). Upper Saddle River, NJ: Prentice-Hall, Inc.

Matson, J. L., & Dilorenzo, T. M. (1984). *Punishment and its alternatives: A new perspective for behavior modification.* NY: Springer Publishing Co.

McGuffin, P. W. (1991). The effect of time-out duration on frequency of aggression in hospitalized children with conduct disorders. *Behavioral Residential Treatment, 6,* 279-288.

National Association of School Psychologists. (1995). *Solve your child's school-related problems.* NY: Harper Perennial.

Newby, R. F., Fischer, M., Roman, M. A. (1991). Parent training for families of children with ADHD. *School Psychology Review, 20,* 252-265.

Patterson, G. R. (1975). *Families: Applications of social learning to family life.* Champaign, IL: Research Press.

Patterson, G. R. (1976). *Living with children: New methods for parents and teachers.* Champaign, IL: Research Press.

Patterson, G. R. (1982). *A social learning approach. Vol. 3. Coercive family process.* Eugene, OR: Castalia Publishing Co.

Patterson, G. R. (1984, November). *Prevention of anitsocial behavior: A problem in three levels.* Paper presented at the meeting of Association for Advancement of Behavior Therapy, Philadelphia, PA. The term "nattering" was coined by J. Reid.

Patterson, G., & Forgatch, M. (1987). *Parents and adolescents living together - Part 1: The basics.* Eugene, OR: Castalia Publishing Co.

Patterson, G., & Forgatch, M. (1989). *Parents and adolescents living together - Part 2: Family problem solving.* Eugene, OR: Castalia Publishing Co.

Polster, R. A., & Dangel, R. F. (Eds.). (1984). *Parent training: Foundations of research and practice.* NY: Guilford Press.

Premack, D. (1959). Toward empirical behavior laws: 1. positive reinforcement. *Psychological Review,* 66, 219-233.

Roberts, M. W. (1982). *Parent handouts 1,2,3.* (Available from Mark Roberts, Idaho State University, Pocatello, ID.)

Roberts, M. W. (1982). Resistance to timeout: Some normative data. *Behavioral Assessment,* 4, 237-246.

Roberts, M. W., McMahon, R. J., Forehand, R., & Humphreys, L. (1978). The effect of parental instruction-giving on child compliance. *Behavior Therapy,* 9, 793-798.

Roberts, M., & Powers, S. (1990). *Behavior Therapy,* 21, 257-271.

Schaefer, C. (1994). *How to talk to your kids about really important things.* San Francisco, CA: Jossey-Bass Publishers.

Schroeder, C. S., Gordon, B. N., & McConnel, P. (1987). Behavior management books for parents. *Journal Of Clinical Child Psychology,* 16, 89-95.

Wierson, M., & Forehand, R. (1994). Parent behavioral training for child noncompliance: Rational, concepts, and effectiveness. *Current Directions in Psychological Science,* 5, 146-150.

White, A., & Bailey, J. (1990). Reducing disruptive behaviors of elementary physical education students with sit and watch. *Journal of Applied Behavior Analysis,* 23, 353-359.

Index

Menu Of Interventions For 46 Problem Behaviors

PROBLEM PARENTS FACE

"Do you want it? Hee, hee, hee!"

Does this remind you of your kids?

To use this *Menu Of Interventions*, look up a particular problem behavior which your child is demonstrating. Study various methods and strategies that you might use to help your child. The list, however, isn't intended to be used without first reading *SOS*, which describes when and how to use these basic methods and techniques for improving behavior.

Aggression — physically aggressive actions including choking, biting, hair pulling, hitting, kicking, pinching, pushing, scratching, slapping, and spitting.

This *Menu Of Interventions* lists more than 46 problem behaviors and over 23 SOS methods for handling and improving these behaviors.

Mental health professionals have told the author that they find this *Menu* especially useful when developing intervention plans for children.

The interventions come from behavior therapy and are research based and clinically tested.

Sample sections from the book, *SOS Help For Emotions*

The purpose of *SOS Help For Emotions* is to help you to decrease and manage your anxiety, anger, or depression and to help you to increase your contentment in daily living. As a result, you can be more successful in attaining your goals, enjoying life more, experiencing better relationships, and maintain better health.

Irrational Beliefs And Self-Talk

Our emotions are largely, but not entirely, controlled by our beliefs, the way we think about problems, and our silent self-talk.

Our rational and irrational beliefs and silent self-talk begin in childhood. We learn these beliefs from our parents and family as well as from peers, friends, society-at-large, and especially mass media. Movies, television, magazines, popular songs, and most types of advertising certainly promote many irrational beliefs and expectations.

Elizabeth, a college freshman with a long history of anorexia, looked emaciated. However, her boyfriend told

Charlie's ABC Analysis Of Anger

A Activating Event

"He said my nose is too big!"

Causes

B Beliefs & Self-Talk

*"He has no right to talk to me that way. He must not, he should not have insulted me. He's a *§æ!±»! fool! What kind of *§æ!±»! person would say such a thing! I-can't-stand him saying that!"*

C Consequences:
Emotional & Behavioral Consequences

*"I am mad! I am angry! I feel like giving that *§æ!±»! a fat nose! Even if he is the boss, I'm going to tell him off and demand an apology!"*

D Dispute

"Wait a minute. I'm making myself mad. He doesn't control my anger; I do. I'm annoyed but I don't have to get angry. I'd prefer that he wouldn't talk to me that way. But I'm responsible for my own anger."

her, *"You look great just as you are now; don't gain a pound!"* He reinforced her irrational beliefs regarding a desirable body as well as her unhealthy eating disorder.

In many cases, we don't adopt irrational beliefs from others; our own peculiar thinking creates irrational beliefs and self-talk statements. After we accept irrational beliefs from others or create our own, *we tend to <u>reindoctrinate</u> ourselves continuously with these irrational beliefs and self-talk statements.* We do this by constantly repeating these beliefs to ourselves and acting on them. Once created, irrational beliefs persist in our conscious awareness as well as in our unconscious unless we actively challenge and modify them.

Carefully focus on the language and words you use when talking with yourself, especially when you feel upset. Your words and language shape your beliefs as well as reveal those beliefs.

Become aware of your irrational beliefs and weaken them by studying and practicing the methods and concepts in *SOS Help For Emotions.* *Weakened irrational beliefs will result in greater contentment and in less anxiety, anger, and depression.*

Emotional Intelligence

Just as people vary in their general intelligence, they vary in their emotional intelligence. *Emotional intelligence is the ability to understand and manage one's emotions.*

Five abilities comprise our emotional intelligence. These abilities include:
- Knowing our emotions
- Managing our emotions
- Recognizing emotions in others
- Managing relationships with others
- Motivating ourselves to achieve our goals

THE BURDEN OF
EXCESS EMOTIONAL BAGGAGE

"I am emotionally <u>worn</u> <u>out</u>! I'm one of those unfortunate people that you hear about. I've burdened myself with lots of irrational self-talk.

While traveling through life, some people carry unnecessarily heavy emotional burdens. Manage your emotions or they will manage both you and your relationships!

Your emotional intelligence contributes more to successful and enjoyable living, than your general intelligence. *Since emotional intelligence is learned rather than inherited, it can be improved. SOS Help For Emotions* teaches specific methods enabling you to better handle your emotions and relationships.

These sample sections are from the book, *SOS Help For Emotions: Managing Anxiety, Anger And Depression* by Lynn Clark, PhD. Read free sample chapters at www.sosprograms.com

DVD Video
SOS
Help For Parents

A Video-Discussion

Parent Education

& Counseling Program

See video clips at www.sosprograms.com

This DVD parent education and counseling program is based on the book, *SOS Help For Parents* and includes the 72 minute DVD, *DVD Video Leader's Guide*, reproducible *Parent Handouts*, *SOS Help For Parents* book, and *Child Management Skills Test* (CMST). All SOS DVD's play internationally, region free.

The SOS DVD program is used by counselors, parent groups, educators, houses of worship, and social service professionals. It is intended for parenting workshops, staff development, in-service training, teacher training, parent counseling, and in college classrooms.

Part One may be viewed by a group or an individual. For Part Two, a discussion leader should guide the discussion following each of the parenting scenes. The easy-to-use *DVD Video Leader's Guide* offers discussion questions and answers for each scene. Enjoyable and user-friendly, the SOS DVD program educates participants in more than 19 behavior management skills. Over 12,000 SOS DVD programs are in use.

DVD Video SOS Ayuda Para Padres

This easy-to-teach program includes the 72 minute DVD (plays internationally, region free), *DVD Video Leader's Guide* in English, reproducible *Parent Handouts* in Spanish, and *SOS Ayuda Para Padres* book. See a sample Spanish video clip at **www.sosprograms.com**

"How To Use Time-Out Effectively"

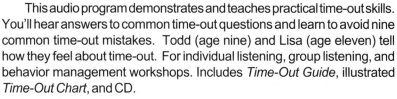

CD Audio Program (67 minutes) by Lynn Clark, Ph.D.

This audio program demonstrates and teaches practical time-out skills. You'll hear answers to common time-out questions and learn to avoid nine common time-out mistakes. Todd (age nine) and Lisa (age eleven) tell how they feel about time-out. For individual listening, group listening, and behavior management workshops. Includes *Time-Out Guide*, illustrated *Time-Out Chart*, and CD.

SOS For Parents Video Scene #17
from Video Leader's Guide

REFUSING APPLE JUICE

Rule #3 Correct some bad behavior (but use mild correction only.)

The bad behavior is knocking the glass of water off the table and loss of self-control.

The mild correction is time-out. Mother provides an example of a "good command" in sending her son to time-out.

Script:

Mother brings apple juice and two crackers to Mitchell who is sitting at the table and demanding cookies.

Mitchell: *"No! I want those cookies!"*

Mom: *"You can have the crackers and apple juice to hold you over to dinner time. It will be ready in about 30 minutes and you may have cookies for dessert."*

Mitchell: *"I don't want any dumb juice!"* (Said as he knocks the glass off the table.)

Mom: *"Time-out! You knocked the glass over. Go now!"*

Mitchell: *"I don't want time-out! I want those cookies!"* (Said as he stomps off to time-out)

Questions, Answers, And Comments:

Q: Which rule or error did mother follow?
    A: Rule #3 Correct some bad behavior (but use mild correction only).

Q: What is the bad behavior?
    A: Knocking the glass over.

Q: What is the correction?
    A: Time-out.

Q: When frustrated in the future, is the child more or less likely to lose control?
    A: Less likely.

Q: Did mother use time-out correctly?
    A: Yes. SOS recommends sending a child to time-out within 10 seconds following the bad behavior and using 10 words or less. Mother sent him to time-out immediately and used only 8 words. Also, mother gave a "good command" in sending her son to time-out.

Suggestions to Presenter: Save a long discussion on time-out until after this video program, and then offer training on time-out.

Technical comments:

Scene demonstrates mild correction of undesirable behavior using time-out. A "good command" is used in sending the child to time-out.

SOS For Parents Video Scene #18
from Video Leader's Guide

SWEEPING THE WALK

Rule #1 Reward good behavior (and do it quickly and often).

The good behavior is trying to help with work.

The reward is a social reward (descriptive praise).

This is also an example of mother setting a good example and daughter imitating mother's behavior.

Script:

Mother and daughter are sweeping the walk in front of their house.

Mom: *"Nicole, I sure like it when you help Mommy sweep the walk. You're doing a good job!"*

Nicole: (Child doesn't say anything, but continues working hard sweeping the walk.)

Questions, Answers, And Comments:

Q: Which rule or error did mother follow?
A: Rule #1 Reward good behavior (and do it quickly and often).

Q: What is the good behavior?
A: Helping mother with work, sweeping the walk.

Q: What is the reward?
A: A social reward (descriptive praise).

Q: Is the child more or less likely to help mother in the future?
A: More likely.

Q: What kind of social rewards did mother use?
A: Smiles, attention, and praise (descriptive praise).

Point To Make: Little Nicole doesn't have to do a perfect job to earn her mother's praise. Parents should reward <u>attempts</u> to do a chore. Also, mother is being a good role-model and Nicole is imitating mother's behavior. Most of what children learn is by observing their parents and others.

Technical Comments:

Scene illustrates positive reinforcement of daughter's desirable behavior, with a social reinforcer (descriptive praise). Scene also demonstrates social imitation (daughter is imitating mother's behavior) and shaping (rewarding an attempt to sweep the walk).

Visit our website at
www.sosprograms.com
Video clips, Audio clips, & Free Resources

ORDER FORM

SOS Programs & Parents Press, PO Box 2180,
Bowling Green, KY 42102-2180 USA

You also can order at our website. Order by phone 1-800-576-1582 toll free, weekdays, 9:00am to 3:00pm Central Standard Time. Can phone 1-270-842-4571. FAX is 270-796-9194. Email is sos@sosprograms.com. Bookstores can order from Ingram and Baker & Taylor. Federal Tax #61-1225614.

For VISA or MasterCard orders, clearly indicate which card, card expiration date, card #, and phone #.

____ Copies of **SOS Help For Emotions** book for $16.00. Not a parenting book. A self-help book for ages 14 to 90 and a handbook for counselors who use cognitive behavior therapy. (2nd Edition Book ISBN-10: 0-935111-52-2; ISBN-13: 978-935111-52-1)

____ Copies of **SOS Help For Parents** book for $16.00. For parents of children two to twelve years old and a handbook for professionals. In English. (3rd Edition Book ISBN-10: 0-0935111-21-2; ISBN-13: 978-0935111-21-7)

____ Copies of Spanish book **SOS Ayuda Con Las Emociones** for $16.00. A self-help book for ages 14 to 90 (& for professionals). (Spanish Book ISBN-10: 0-935111-75-1; ISBN-13: 978-0-935111-75-0)

____ Copies of Spanish book **SOS Ayuda Para Padres** for $16.00. For parents of children 2 to 12 years old (& for professionals). (Spanish Book ISBN-10: 0-935111-47-6; ISBN-13: 978-0-935111-47-7)

____ Copies of **"How To Use Time-Out Effectively"** CD audio program (67 minutes), Time-Out Guide, Time-Out Chart, and CD for $16.00. For parents and parent workshops. (Audio ISBN: 0-935111-32-8)

____ **DVD Video SOS Help For Parents** education program & Kit for $180.00. Free shipping within USA. Program includes 72 minute DVD (plays internationally, region free), DVD Video Leader's Guide, Parent Handouts, SOS Help For Parents book, and additional materials. (SOS DVD Kit ISBN: 0-935111-38-7) Visit our website and see video clips. See description on pp. 205 - 208.

____ **DVD Video SOS Ayuda Para Padres** program Kit for $180.00. Free shipping within USA. Includes 72 minute DVD (plays internationally, region free), DVD Video Leader's Guide, SOS Ayuda Para Padres book, Spanish handouts, etc. (Spanish DVD ISBN: 0-935111-48-4) Visit our website and see a two minute video sample in Spanish.

ORDER FORM Continued

Orders from individuals must be prepaid by check or credit card. Agencies may FAX their purchase orders. We pay any taxes. Federal Tax #61-1225614.

If not satisfied, I understand that I may return any SOS materials for a refund.

Mailing Label — Please Print Clearly

Name: _____

Address: _____

City: _____ State: _____ Zip: _____

Credit Card Check One: ☐ VISA ☐ MasterCard

Credit card Expiration Date _____

Account # _____

_____
Print name as it appears on card.

Daytime Phone (_____) _____
(Telephone number is necessary if credit card is used.)

Shipping: Include $6.00 shipping for first book or audio CD and $1.00 shipping for each additional book or audio CD. Shipping is by US Air Mail or UPS.

_____ *Quantity Discounts:* **If you are ordering at least five books, deduct 20% from the cost of the books. You may mix titles of books & CD's to total five.** The discount applies only to books & CD's. *Many professionals make SOS books available to clients when they most need them - immediately! Counselors also loan SOS books with a $16 deposit. Clients keep books or return them.*

_____ I am a counselor, educator, or professional.

Foreign country orders: All orders must be prepaid in US funds **with credit cards, money orders or checks drawn on US banks.** For Canadian shipping double US shipping rates.

Foreign editions of *SOS Help For Parents* or *SOS Help For Emotions* - call regarding availability. All available foreign editions are $16.00. Also, they may be ordered through the Amazon website of the country and language in which you are interested.

Visit our website at
www.sosprograms.com
Video clips, Audio clips, & Free Resources

ORDER FORM

SOS Programs & Parents Press, PO Box 2180,
Bowling Green, KY 42102-2180 USA

You also can order at our website. Order by phone 1-800-576-1582
toll free, weekdays, 9:00am to 3:00pm Central Standard Time. Can
phone 1-270-842-4571. FAX is 270-796-9194. Email is
sos@sosprograms.com. Bookstores can order from Ingram and
Baker & Taylor. Federal Tax #61-1225614.
     For VISA or MasterCard orders, clearly indicate which card, card
expiration date, card #, and phone #.

___ Copies of **SOS Help For Emotions** book for $16.00. Not a
parenting book. A self-help book for ages 14 to 90 and a handbook for
counselors who use cognitive behavior therapy. (2nd Edition Book ISBN-
10: 0-935111-52-2; ISBN-13: 978-935111-52-1)

___ Copies of **SOS Help For Parents** book for $16.00. For parents of
children two to twelve years old and a handbook for professionals. In
English. (3rd Edition Book ISBN-10: 0-0935111-21-2; ISBN-13: 978-0935111-
21-7)

___ Copies of Spanish book **SOS Ayuda Con Las Emociones** for $16.00.
A self-help book for ages 14 to 90 (& for professionals). (Spanish Book
ISBN-10: 0-935111-75-1; ISBN-13: 978-0-935111-75-0)

___ Copies of Spanish book **SOS Ayuda Para Padres** for $16.00. For
parents of children 2 to 12 years old (& for professionals). (Spanish Book
ISBN-10: 0-935111-47-6; ISBN-13: 978-935111-47-7)

___ Copies of **"How To Use Time-Out Effectively"** CD audio program (67
minutes), Time-Out Guide, Time-Out Chart, and CD for $16.00. For
parents and parent workshops. (Audio ISBN: 0-935111-32-8)

___ **DVD Video SOS Help For Parents** education program & Kit for $180.00.
Free shipping within USA. Program includes 72 minute DVD (plays
internationally, region free), DVD Video Leader's Guide, Parent
Handouts, SOS Help For Parents book, and additional materials. (SOS
DVD Kit ISBN: 0-935111-38-7) Visit our website and see video clips.
See description on pp. 205 - 208.

___ **DVD Video SOS Ayuda Para Padres** program Kit for $180.00. Free
shipping within USA. Includes 72 minute DVD (plays internationally,
region free), DVD Video Leader's Guide, SOS Ayuda Para Padres book,
Spanish handouts, etc. (Spanish DVD ISBN: 0-935111-48-4) Visit our
website and see a two minute video sample in Spanish.

ORDER FORM Continued

Orders from individuals must be prepaid by check or credit card. Agencies may FAX their purchase orders. We pay any taxes. Federal Tax #61-1225614.

If not satisfied, I understand that I may return any SOS materials for a refund.

Mailing Label — Please Print Clearly

Name: _____

Address: _____

City: _____ State: _____ Zip: _____

Credit Card Check One: ☐ VISA   ☐ MasterCard

Credit card Expiration Date _____

Account # _____

_____
Print name as it appears on card.

Daytime Phone (_____) _____
(Telephone number is necessary if credit card is used.)

Shipping: Include $6.00 shipping for first book or audio CD and $1.00 shipping for each additional book or audio CD. Shipping is by US Air Mail or UPS.

_____ *Quantity Discounts:* **If you are ordering at least five books, deduct 20% from the cost of the books. You may mix titles of books & CD's to total five.** The discount applies only to books & CD's. *Many professionals make SOS books available to clients when they most need them - immediately! Counselors also loan SOS books with a $16 deposit. Clients keep books or return them.*

_____ I am a counselor, educator, or professional.

Foreign country orders: All orders must be prepaid in US funds **with credit cards, money orders or checks drawn on US banks**. For Canadian shipping double US shipping rates.

Foreign editions of *SOS Help For Parents* or *SOS Help For Emotions* - call regarding availability. All available foreign editions are $16.00. Also, they may be ordered through the Amazon website of the country and language in which you are interested.